CW01661404

How Did I Get Here?

How Did I Get Here?

A MEMOIR | VOLUME 3

Love Is the Answer!

GORDON CRAIGIE

First published in Scotland in 2026 by
iScot Media, 4 The Kirklands, Torbrex,
Stirling, FK7 9BF

Copyright © Gordon Craigie 2026

The moral right of Gordon Craigie to be identified as the Author
of this Work has been asserted by him in accordance with the
Copyright, Designs and Patents Act 1988.

All rights reserved. No part of this publication may be reproduced,
distributed, or transmitted in any form or by any means, electronic
or mechanical, including photocopy, recording, or any information
storage and retrieval system, without first obtaining the written
permission of the copyright owner.

The End
Words and Music by John Lennon and Paul McCartney
Copyright © 1969 Sony Music Publishing (US) LLC and
MPL Communications, Inc. in the United States
Copyright Renewed
All Rights for the world excluding the United States Administered
by Sony Music Publishing (US) LLC, 424 Church Street, Suite 1200,
Nashville, TN 37219
International Copyright Secured All Rights Reserved
Reprinted by Permission of Hal Leonard LLC

ISBN: 978-1-8382500-5-8
ebook ISBN: 978-1-8382500-8-9

Edited by Angela Valente *www.aveditorial.scot*
Typeset by Laura Kincaid *www.tenthousand.co.uk*
Cover design by Robert Mulligan
Cover image by Ian Bain

This book is dedicated to four very special people:

To my late mother, father and brother:
Ellen (Ella) Cooper Craigie, née McIntosh, 1922–1999
Thomas (Tom) Crawford Craigie, 1926–2011
Thomas (Tommy) Craigie, 1946–1989
without whom this book would not have been possible, and for making my journey to adulthood everything that I could have wished for.

And to Angela Valente, my wife and soulmate, without whose constant encouragement and belief this book would never have been written, and for making me complete.

Grateful thanks to Ken McDonald for inviting me into the iScot family and for his support and encouragement, allowing me to be myself as a writer.

Contents

Introduction

You may experience a sense of déjà vu reading the following few paragraphs – I suppose it all depends on whether you've read, or remembered, either or both of the previous books! The only way to know for certain is to read on…

In the introduction to *How Did I Get Here?: Volume 1 – Rebel Without a Clue!* I said:

> *I never set out to write a funny book but, apparently, it is! However, you, as the reader, will be best placed to judge that…*

Wise words, and so many readers confirmed that it was indeed funny – in a good way! – that it only encouraged me to move the story along by another 20 years with *How Did I Get Here?: Volume 2 – Raging Against the Machine!*, so blame them!

And since there was a similarly pleasing and humbling response from readers to that book, here we are again jumping another 20 or so years forward with *How Did I Get Here?: Volume 3 – Love Is the Answer!*

If you read *Rebel Without a Clue!*, then you'll remember what my motivations were for writing it – and if you didn't read it, why not? *Raging Against the Machine!* and *Love Is the Answer!* will make a whole lot more sense if you do! Both of those books are still available – check out *www.gordoncraigie.scot/books* for all the different ways you can buy them.

You'll also remember that the lyrics from two songs in particular summed up the whole project for me: "In My Life" by the Beatles and "Once in a Lifetime" by Talking Heads.

Those words still resonate strongly with me, and everything in this book is still about the people, places and experiences that have shaped me. And the writing of it, once again, hopefully, takes me another wee bit closer to understanding for myself the answer to the question that started this whole thing off: *How Did I Get Here?*

PROLOGUE

In my life (act III)

(2025)

Ah, here we go again then, completing the trilogy, but not before a bit more of that déjà vu stuff…

In the first book, I wrote:

> *It's confession time – this book was originally conceived, and the first draft written, in the spring of 2012, but is only being completed now, the summer of 2020 – I did mention more than once during the book that there's no point in rushing these things!*

So, originally I thought I was writing one book – and that was a huge deal for me, as it would be for anybody – but, as evidenced by the fact that you're reading these words, it turns out that it was a much bigger project than I imagined, and this book is actually completing the trilogy! In Volume 2, we meandered through another 20 years, and now Volume 3 will bring us up to the year time stood still, 2020. But who knows? Maybe in time the trilogy will expand too… I find the prospect of a four-part trilogy quite appealing actually!

In Volume 1, the subtitle, *Rebel Without a Clue!*, was intended to convey that I was telling the story of a daft wee laddie doing his best to navigate his way through the opportunities, and obstacles, that we all experience to a greater or lesser extent while growing up. I had a fantastic childhood, surrounded by love and security, and the process of simply writing many of my recollections down made me appreciate that all the more. One reader commented that the book was "a couthy read – warm, funny and nostalgic" and was "clearly written with love – it glows from the pages – touching his family, his passion for football, for music, for his teachers and mentors, and, of course, his wife". I'm so pleased that all came across.

For the second volume, I went with *Raging Against the Machine!* as the subtitle because I think that adult life, and the world of work especially, is designed to make us live our lives in a predetermined way, and if you were paying attention in *Rebel Without a Clue!*, then you'd have understood that this particular clueless rebel widnae take kindly, or submit willingly, tae that! Again, most of that book was drafted in 2012, and I pretty much tried to keep to my original thoughts, only adding in 2022 updates where appropriate.

And so we arrive at Volume 3, which is intriguingly (?) subtitled *Love Is the Answer!* – which may be self-explanatory, but, if not, you'll have to wait another few hundred pages to find out exactly why. Volume 1 was mainly about the innocence of schooldays and growing up, while Volume 2 moved on to the idiocy of the world of work and establishment pressures designed to make us all conform to some predetermined norm – determined by who knows whom for who knows why! Now, Volume 3 reveals how our rebel without a clue

– that'll be me! – emerges from his period of raging against the machine to arrive at… well, that would spoil this book, wouldn't it?

Once again, the first five chapters were originally drafted in 2012, but the rest of this book was written between 2023 and 2025 – I'll give you a not-very-subtle clue later on as to when the handover takes place…

CHAPTER 1

Déjà vu all over again

(1959–2002, reprise!)

Final piece of déjà vu – for now – honest! Though I must admit I'm really quite partial to including things as a *reprise* – it makes me think I'm channelling Sergeant Pepper.

Well, here we are yet again. I knew this was going to happen, and, in fact, I predicted it at the end of Volume 1:

> *So there's more to come, another book's worth in fact,*
> *that'll pick up where this one leaves off and probably*
> *also include some things that I've forgotten from this one,*
> *maybe presented as some kind of dream sequence?*

At that point, I obviously hadn't realised there were actually another two books to come. You may recall that I quickly discounted the "dream sequence" idea, mainly because I had absolutely no idea how to pull that off. It may well be worth a try in some future project, but as I've said before, it's just easier to try and string together some of the stories that I knew I'd forgotten to include as soon as the manuscript had gone off to the printer – twice! Fear not, dear reader, we'll return to our almost-chronological narrative in Chapter 2, but for now, once again, let's go back in time…

We might as well start off with a few random football stories, since so many readers commented on how little I'd mentioned the beautiful game…

I've previously recounted my happy days playing for my brother's pub team, romantically (?) named AFC Station because we were sponsored by the Station Hotel in Carnoustie and the "AFC" bit just seemed cool. Anyway, our wee club was ambitious and looking for a bigger challenge than that which the Arbroath & District League provided so we applied to join the Dundee Sunday Morning League. We really should have read the runes about this adventure when one of the clubs objected to having to travel to Carnoustie once a season – a whole 12 miles! – so the league insisted that we play all our games in Dundee instead. We adopted Dawson Park in Broughty Ferry as our home ground as it was the closest for us and couldn't be objected to by our reluctant fellow travellers – though, clearly, non-travellers would be a more accurate description.

The season went really well, and playing against new teams was both refreshing and interesting. In fact, it went so well that we were top of the league with four games left to play and looking likely to win the title. However, the team that had objected to our entry in the first place then raised an objection to something else – I don't remember what it was, but, in reality, it was probably nothing! – so our officials were called before a committee meeting to "discuss" the situation.

Maybe this is the time to add in the minor detail that the team objecting to our presence had won the title for several seasons in succession and were looking likely to finish second behind us… oh, and we'd already beaten them… twice!

Apparently, the meeting was a farce, with the league office-bearers in cahoots with our opponents and clearly looking to get rid of us pesky outsiders. At a certain point, our guys stood up and said, "If they want the title that badly, let them have it – we resign," and left the room. So that was that – so near and yet so far! It's a shame, as a league winner's medal would've been nice, but our officials acted on principle and were entirely justified. The people who ran the other team are well-known "characters" in Dundee to this day... he said enigmatically.

Dad used to come and watch a lot of our games, but it was always a bone of contention between him and Tommy as Tommy didn't like Dad coming. I don't know why; I never knew why. Maybe he thought Dad being there somehow cramped his style? No idea. I mean, he wasn't even playing, so he couldn't say he was being put off or anything. But I liked it when Dad came, and obviously he wanted to see his younger son playing football even if his elder son was only playing silly beggars!

Anyway, one Sunday we were playing at Dawson, and our referee was the legendarily incompetent Willie X – name withheld to protect the guilty! For starters, the pitch was genuinely unplayable – it was frozen solid and had shards of ice in the centre circle and goalmouths! When we forcibly pointed this out to him, the bold Willie confidently declared, "Aye, ye'll jist hae tae be careful there lads..."

So, at no inconsiderable danger to life and limb, the game went ahead, and the begloved Willie refereed the entire game from within the centre circle, carefully tiptoeing around the stalagmites no doubt, which maybe at least partially explained why many of his decisions were even more incomprehensible than usual. Or maybe it was just because he seemed to be particularly friendly with our opponents, who certainly got more than their fair share of decisions. Offsides in their favour were confidently called from his less-than-textbook position at the halfway line, free kicks were awarded to them quite randomly while he happily ignored some brutal challenges on our players. It was as perfect an example of biased refereeing as you're ever likely to witness. After yours truly had been kicked upside down for the umpteenth time with no free kick awarded, Dad felt the need to intervene on his wee boy's behalf.

"Come on, ref – play fair," came the shout from the touchline.

This gratuitous outburst was too much for Willie to handle. He blew his whistle and, for the only time in the game, left the sanctity of the centre circle and stomped angrily across the icy turf to confront my dad, who was standing a good distance away from Tommy and our other officials and substitutes.

"What's your name?" he demanded.

"That's none of your business," Dad replied. "I'm just here to watch a game of football, which you're ruining with biased refereeing."

"What do you mean?"

"It's simply not possible for every decision in a game to be given in only one direction, and that laddie's been fouled persistently. Somebody's going to get seriously hurt, and it's going to be your fault."

"I want you to leave the park."

"What?"

"I want you to leave the park immediately or I'm abandoning the game."

"This is a public park, and you can't make me do anything."

At that rebuff, Willie turned towards Tommy and our boys. "I want that man removed from the park."

Tommy looked towards Dad then looked back at Willie and, without missing a beat, calmly replied, "He's not with us. I've never seen him before in my life."

At this Willie admitted defeat, huffily marched back to his centre circle and restarted the game with a free kick to our opponents, despite no offence having been committed prior to his tantrum!

We must've played particularly well in the circumstances as the game finished 0–0, despite Willie's best efforts, and we all had a good laugh about it afterwards. The look on his coupon when he was faced down by my dad – priceless! Dad couldn't believe what he'd witnessed.

OK, enough football already – let's return to some feline fun and frolics! I mentioned our furry little black-and-white bundle of joy, Stushie, in the previous book, but on rereading that part, I realised that there were so many stories of the wee man that I hadn't recorded. Yes, I had detailed the unsuccessful attempt to put him on a lead and also his "not now, Cato" moment when he louped at me and destroyed the video cabinet, and a few other bits, but I'd obviously decided that you'd probably had enough pussycatting at that stage. Now you've had time to recover though, here's some more…

Stushie, probably like most cats, seemed to like hiding. One evening, while I was getting everything ready for football training, my packed kitbag was sitting out in the hall while I finished off whatever I was doing. When the time came to leave, I grabbed the bag and went out to the car, swinging the bag into the passenger seat as usual. I still don't know what made me look inside, but I opened the bag and there he was, curled up with his eyes tightly shut and that "if I don't see you, then you're not there" expression. He looked more than a wee bit grumpy and disappointed when I hauled him out and deposited him back in the house, but football dressing rooms can be fairly unforgiving places, and I can only imagine the abuse I would've received if I'd turned up with my cat in my bag – little rascal!

In 1997, when we moved into our Dundee house, we left Stush with my parents for a few days until we'd had the furniture delivered and sorted out a little of the inevitable moving-in chaos. Introducing him to his new home was a fascinating experience and a real insight into cat psychology. As soon as we let him out of his travel box, he immediately walked purposefully around the edge of every room on the ground floor before warily making his way upstairs and repeating his reconnaissance mission. Then he adopted the windowsill halfway up the stairs as his preferred vantage point for the next few days – from there, he could see both downstairs and upstairs and knew nothing could come from behind him. Amazing to watch. But, like us, he quickly settled down and treated the place like he owned it... which, obviously, he did!

Once he was introduced to the great outdoors, he would demand to be let out a few times a day, but he never wandered far and was usually back on a windowsill demanding re-entry quite quickly! His absolute peak of spoiled behaviour though had to be his insistence on being towelled down and having each paw individually dried after coming back in from the rain. And yes, guilty as charged – I had made him like that!

He continually refined his ability to locate the strangest places to hide – one day both Angela and I had each searched every room in the house for him, twice, and there was no sign of the little sod. We knew he hadn't gone out, but where on earth was he hiding?

On my third visit to our spare bedroom, just as I was about to leave the room, something drew my attention to the bed – nothing obvious, but I just had a feeling. I ran my hand over the perfectly flat duvet and felt an almost imperceptible lump – yes, his lordship had somehow managed to get himself under the duvet and into the middle of the bed without leaving a wrinkle as evidence! Just like with the sports bag incident, when I pulled the duvet back, there he was all curled up with his eyes firmly shut.

I know this is a lot of cat stuff, but, honestly, there was never a dull moment with that wee beastie. If he was bored, he would wander around the house meowing and looking for mischief, and most of the time I would be his target, especially if I was sitting in the living room relaxing. He would slowly, innocently, walk into the room with his tail raised, appearing disinterested in whatever I was doing, then he would surreptitiously get close enough to flick out a paw and batter my leg before haring off in a very "chase me, chase me", "play with me – I wanna play" manner... and I, far more often than not, would willingly oblige.

Everybody who has ever had a pet will know that they're an integral part of the family, and Stushie was exactly that for almost 15 years. When we noticed that he was a bit lethargic and had been off his food for a couple of days, we took him to the vet – who just happened to be our next-door neighbour – and she advised us to take him to another practice because they had a particular piece of scanning equipment that may help to diagnose what was wrong. Unfortunately, the diagnosis wasn't good. The vet told us that his kidneys were failing and that he was in a lot of pain, and that the kindest thing to do was to let him go. Honestly, I'm tearing up just writing this, and it was 25 years ago! What a hellish decision to have to make, but we couldn't see him suffer. We were both devastated, as was my dad, and we had a very emotional wee ceremony in our garden, burying him in a shady corner. Stushie was a great companion and added so much to our family, and he's still missed…

There are a few work-related anecdotes that I probably should've included previously, so now's as good a time as any to finally squeeze them in…

Now, when I was at school, both as a pupil and a teacher, if it was snowing, you simply trudged through the snow to and from school. Maybe some of the teachers who lived further away wouldn't make it in, and sometimes the school buses for pupils who lived in deepest, darkest Angus wouldn't run, but for the rest of us, nothing changed. By the time the 1990s rolled around however, health and safety practices had moved on apace, and we witnessed the advent of "snow days". A snow day would see the closure, on safety grounds, of schools and colleges, at the direction of the headteacher or local authority, or of the college principal, and these decisions would be communicated to the great unwashed via the local radio stations, in our case Radio Tay.

I never used to listen to Radio Tay, but it quickly became essential listening in winter anytime the snow had arrived or was threatened. My radio alarm was usually set for 7 a.m., and one snowy Friday morning, I was listening to closures being announced all over Angus, Dundee, Fife and Perthshire, drifting in and out of sleepy consciousness but becoming very alert at any mention of "Dundee".

Now, the sensible thing to do would've been to get up and get ready to leave earlier than usual for work because, closure or no closure, the snow was bad and driving would be slower than usual. But the cosiness of being tucked up under the duvet awaiting the "inevitable" announcement was definitely winning as we ticked past 7.15, 7.30, 8 a.m., until finally, around 8.40, I heard the words I'd been eagerly, or drowsily, anticipating – "Dundee College is closed…" – and I instinctively snapped the off button and settled in for another couple of hours of snoozing.

Around 10.30 or 11 a.m., there was an exchange of phone calls with my gym-going buddies, who were also benefiting from a snow day, and we bravely trachled our way through the snow to Carnoustie Leisure Centre for a couple of hours playing head tennis before, probably, heading to the pub – happy days!

What I hadn't realised at the time was that when I'd hit the off button, I'd missed the rest of the sentence, "… to students, but open as usual for staff", a fact that my colleagues were only too keen to tell me on the Monday! I was, however, unabashed at this revelation, as that was an illogical and stupid decision anyway. Besides, nobody really noticed and nobody cared.

By the time I'd reached the dizzy heights of Project Lauder however, snow days became a little more complicated.

While I was still living in Carnoustie, it had started to snow quite heavily on the Sunday, and by Monday morning, Radio Tay was broadcasting a direct instruction from Tayside Police saying that the road from Carnoustie to Dundee was blocked and that under no circumstances was anyone to be allowed through. I phoned my boss, John, who laughed and said he was looking at green fields from his office window, but he accepted that I was telling the truth and that he'd see me once it was safe to travel again.

The next morning, the news had changed, and while it was now possible to leave Carnoustie, it was impossible to get through Dundee. Another phone call, more laughter, let's see what tomorrow brings.

By Wednesday, the update was that Carnoustie was fine, Dundee was better, but no travel was being allowed beyond Perth – another phone call, more muted laughter this time as the white stuff had finally started to fall in Dunfermline and, again, let's see what the position is tomorrow. We didn't get that far as John phoned me later that night to say that West Fife was now cut off so… another day off, magic!

However… if you remember the culture of fear at Lauder College, I felt I had to show willing on the Friday, so I set off on what turned out to be a treacherous journey to Dunfermline, eventually arriving around 10.30 a.m. having taken almost three hours to get there – twice as long as usual – with the section from the Friarton Bridge at Perth to Dunfermline being particularly tricky. On Friday mornings, the principal – remember her, Beelzebub? – requested, or "insisted", that her senior staff all shared coffee together in the college's Training Restaurant, and when I walked in, all my colleagues started cheering and applauding… only slightly embarrassing! However, she who must be obeyed had a face like fizz, so I was more than a little concerned when she made her way across to speak to me a short time later.

Disconcertingly, as she approached, a rarely seen smile appeared on her frosty coupon, and she said, "Morning, Gordon. It's good to see you back, and thank you for making the effort today – I know it's still quite wild further north."

Jeezy peeps, I certainly wasn't expecting that. John told me later that she was probably smiling because my having made it through from as far away as Carnoustie, and having come across the bridge at Perth, had just blasted a hole into her assistant principal's excuse of not being able to come in from Perth – she did like a victim!

Now, back to the actual "work" aspect of the world of work...

I previously commented on some common misconceptions about lecturing in a college, where people generally think it must be an easy life because "the students actually want to be there". That may be true for some, and I certainly met many incredibly motivated people who worked extremely hard to achieve whatever it was they were aiming for. Further education is absolutely essential for what may be termed "second chance" education, for people who, for whatever reason, didn't do well at school but with a bit of maturity and life experience behind them return to the classroom to get the qualifications they've belatedly realised are important to them. It's the very essence of lifelong learning and should be freely available to anybody at any time in their life, in my opinion. And then there are the ones who are only there because they have to be, like the day-release apprentices. Now, don't get me wrong, many of them are equally motivated and hardworking... but many are not!

One outstanding example of this latter genre was a group of wannabe brickies I taught at Dundee College during the block-release phase of their apprenticeship. "Block release" meant they attended college full-time for a "block" of six weeks.

The guys – they were all male – were probably happy enough when they were in the workshops or outside mixing cement and laying bricks and so on, but when it came to their core skills classes… it would be fair to say that they were generally not so keen! Amongst the general bleating, their most common refrains were: "Why are we doing this? What do we need this for? I hated this at school!" With this particular group – there were only nine of them – every lesson was a battle to get them to do anything at all, and getting all of them to do something meaningful – and at the same time! – was almost impossible.

One day, I was teaching them about ratio and proportion when the usual, and predictable, "Why do we need this?" shout went up.

"Well, if you're mixing sand and cement and water, you need to know the ratios to get the mix right."

"No we dinnae. If it's no' right, we jist chuck in anither bittie sand or cement or watter until it is right!"

Hmm.

Another day, we were attempting estimation, and I thought I was on solid ground by saying they needed to know how to estimate to make sure they had the right amounts of materials on the job.

"The gaffer dis that."

Thinking I was playing a trump card, I replied, "But what if you're doing a homer?"

"We jist buy big bags an' if we dinnae yaise it on this job, we'll yaise it on the next."

Sometimes it's just easier to admit defeat.

One of this ensemble – let's call him Davie – was a particularly good source of material for illustrating some of the challenges involved. He was most definitely the leader of this particular pack and feared/respected (delete as appropriate!) by the others. Other than the fact he wouldn't actually do any work, I liked him – he had a cheeky personality, quite gallus, and could actually be very entertaining. Anyway, a couple of weeks into the teaching block, he disappeared and the boys told me he was "in the jail"! When he reappeared after another couple of weeks, completely unabashed by his experience, I asked him what had happened…

"I caught this guy in bed wi ma burd, so I got my samurai sword fae under the bed and attacked him."

We never did get an explanation as to why he routinely kept a samurai sword under his bed, but given that it all sounded like a pretty serious offence to me, I asked him why he wasn't still in jail.

"I've got tae go tae the coort next month, cos I'm pleadin' self-defence."

As his victim had been naked at the time of the offence, I was tempted to ask him what exactly he was defending himself against.

Another time, when we'd packed up a few minutes early and they were just milling around restlessly and pleading to go, just to make conversation and deflect their impatience, I told Davie that I liked the leather jacket he was wearing. He seemed quite chuffed by the compliment and said, "D'ye like it? Ye can hae it fir a tenner. It's brand new – there's jist a wee tear on this shoulder whaur the tag came aff."

Thanks but no thanks, Davie!

And finally, honest, a few wee stories to be filed under "holiday adventures"…

In Volume 2, I told various stories from our visit to Canada back in 1995 but, inexplicably, forgot to mention one of our favourite ever experiences, from one of our explorations of downtown Toronto. One of my cousins had told us that

Yonge Street was the longest street in the world, so we felt compelled to check it out. It was originally claimed to go from the shore of Lake Ontario in Toronto to Lake Simcoe – almost 1,200 miles! – but, following various redefinitions, it's now reckoned to be around 34 miles... still pretty long to me!

Anyway, we decided to explore a bit one gloriously sunny morning, and around noon we stumbled across a large, and steadily growing, crowd of people outside what turned out to be a Virgin Megastore – remember them? I fought my way through far enough to see a sign in the window which read, "Red Hot Chili Peppers appearing here live today at 12.30 p.m." – fantastic! Everyone appeared to be looking across the road, and we saw that a temporary stage had been set up, so we navigated to a decent viewing position and settled in for the wait.

Rock stars being rock stars, 12.30 stretched out to at least 1.30, and it really was uncomfortably hot in the blazing midday sunshine – as we've already covered in some detail, not the ideal conditions for two wee peely-wally Scots to be caught in unprepared.

Eventually, the band turned up and played an excellent set for around 30–40 minutes. Remember, this was 1995 and way, way before the Peppers had forsaken the classic rock 'n' roll lifestyle to become clean-living, born-again, macrobiotic health freaks, so it was fair to say that they were fuelled by a wee bit more than caffeine... The singer, Anthony Kiedis, was swinging around the scaffolding supporting the makeshift stage and blamed their lateness on the Canadian authorities delaying their entry to the country due to "previous drug-related offences". Thankfully, they'd only been delayed and not denied entry, and it was quite surreal for us to see one of our favourite bands, then and now, so close-up and so completely unexpectedly. So, apart from a bit of sunburn (!), a not-too-shabby day out on Yonge Street – good times!

We also enjoyed a couple of city breaks during the latter half of the 1990s that didn't go entirely to plan. One was in Istanbul during our Easter holidays, and in the sure and certain (?) knowledge that April in a Mediterranean country would be warm, we had packed accordingly. On the night before we were due to leave, I decided to double-check on the weather – I think I was expecting to see wall-to-wall sunshine forecast – but the only way to check on a relatively obscure destination like Istanbul was to look it up on Teletext... remember that? Anyway, it took some time for the Teletext pages to work their way through the alphabet from wherever they were when I tuned in, but, eventually, up came Istanbul... and the temperature was -3°C... whit? I thought I must've made a mistake, so I sat (im)patiently waiting for it to roll round again... Nope, I was right enough: -3°C.

I told Angela, and her immediate reaction was, understandably enough, that I must be mistaken, so we both sat and waited for it to come round again, and again: -3°C! Despite this confirmation, we were still a little bit dubious but decided we'd better take heavier coats "just in case"...

On arrival in Istanbul, we were whisked off to our hotel – a fairly prestigious-looking high-rise in Taksim Square – by bus and immediately headed off to bed as it was almost midnight and we'd been travelling for eight hours or so. Our room was fairly high up and enjoyed a great view over the city. At some point, we were both woken up by what sounded like some wailing and off-key singing, which I sleepily dismissed as being someone drunk outside – forgetting that we were something like eight floors up! We later realised it had been a call to prayer at the Taksim Mosque at around five o'clock in the morning, and there was a great big television screen relaying this on the mosque wall, high up and right outside our window...

After breakfast, suitably refreshed, we headed out into a bright and sunny Istanbul morning to walk the short distance downhill to the nearest famous sight – so famous I can't remember what it was! As soon as we stepped outside, we realised we'd been fooled by seeing the bright conditions from our centrally-heated hotel, as it was absolutely freezing, so we quickly headed back in to put more clothes on.

Take 2, and as we headed down the hill towards the waterfront, it started to rain, heavily, with a fiercely freezing wind blowing the rain straight at us. For the second time, we beat a hasty retreat to dry off, heat up and revise our plans. Thankfully, that was the only rain we had, so we were able to navigate the next few chilly days by basically wearing every stitch of clothing we'd brought with us!

The next morning, as we left the hotel, we were confronted by thousands of people lining Taksim Square to view what we eventually discovered was some kind of military parade involving soldiers, armoured vehicles, barking dogs, and special forces abseiling from helicopters, all to the cheering delight of the Turkish citizens. We hadn't realised that Taksim Square was so important, a fact that would come back to bite us later.

On our last day, we decided to take a river cruise so we could see what the city looked like from the Bosphorus Strait. Our research had concluded that this was a round-trip, but quite typically for us, our research turned out to be wrong. We realised there were several stop-offs along the route, and when everybody we recognised from our hotel got off at one point, we did wonder what they were doing and how they would get back.

Anyway, at that point, we were still recovering from an unbelievably funny experience with a white-jacketed, black-bow-tied waiter onboard who bore more than a passing resemblance to Albert Einstein. We'd ordered a couple of coffees from Albert, and when he returned with the brews, I handed him whatever note I had and waited for my change. It's probably worth explaining that Albert spoke no English, and I spoke no Turkish. He handed me something and smiled from beneath his wayward tache, but I just looked at the change then looked at him because he was clearly trying to diddle us. Unperturbed, Albert topped up the change, I looked at it then looked at him, still with my hand out. Still unperturbed, he proffered more change into my palm, which I looked at then looked up at him – this time because I now had more money in my hand than I'd started with! He was still smiling and about to hand over even more when I stopped him, said thank you and withdrew my hand. He smiled, bowed and wandered off, apparently completely happy with what had just taken place. I really don't think he was "at it"; I think he just offered people what he thought might be correct and if they accepted it, then fine. If they didn't, then he'd offer more. But a very funny experience.

We continued on our merry way, but when the boat reached the next stop, it became clear that it was the end of the line – c'mon, get aff! It then transpired that the boat was now in situ for another four hours and that we would be too late for our airport bus by the time we got back to the hotel...

After much scrambling around and head scratching, we eventually spotted a much smaller boat, which was due to leave imminently, which would at least get us onto the right side of the river, from where we could get a bus to Taksim Square – phew! This wee boat didn't fill us with much confidence mind, as it had duckboards to keep the passengers' feet dry from the murky water that was somehow finding its way into the boat! To balance out this fear, the other passengers were all housewives who presumably used this "water bus" every day without coming to a soggy end. Anyway, it all worked out well in the end – we easily found a bus on the other side and returned to our hotel with plenty of time to spare. So much so, in fact, that Angela decided we had enough time to return to the Grand Bazaar to pick up some trinket she hadn't quite made her mind up on when we previously visited. Well, what could possibly go wrong?

When we got to the stall she wanted to visit, she still couldn't make her mind up, and after much humming and hawing, she decided that whatever it was wasn't exactly what she wanted anyway. We hailed a taxi and immediately got into an absolute gridlock of a traffic jam. Now, this bonus trip to the Grand Bazaar was always going to be tight, despite Angela's confident declaration of "plenty time", so this hold-up was more than a wee bit worrying. But there was nothing we could do, and eventually we were resigned to probably having to get a taxi to the airport as we were well past the departure time of our bus before we even arrived at the hotel.

However, luck was on our side as the bus was still there, and we were greeted by an ever-so-slightly stressed tour guide barking, "Hurry up, you two," as we rushed inside to collect our luggage. Back on the bus, as we made our apologies, the guide explained that the traffic jam had been caused by roads being closed due to the President (the actual president of Turkey!) visiting our hotel that afternoon – we go to all the best places!

Without wishing to pick on my extremely well-organised and meticulous other half, the next holiday tale of woe also rests firmly on her wee shoulders, as all the organisation and booking for this one was down to her – another city break, this time in Madrid.

We wandered wearily into our city centre hotel just before midnight and were warmly greeted by the reception staff – so far, so good. As the receptionist tapped away on her keyboard, we could see her expression slowly changing and, eventually, she said that we didn't have a booking. Wait, what? Angela fished out her paperwork, the receptionist scrutinised it then began furiously tapping away again before confirming that we didn't have a booking. Angela had booked it through Expedia, and although they'd happily taken our money, they apparently hadn't confirmed the booking with the hotel – thanks very much, Expedia! The girl was very understanding and keen to help, so she explained our situation to the manager, and the two of them tapped away again for a bit, then he disappeared into a back office where we could see him on the phone. When he returned, he told us he had negotiated for us to stay that night at their sister hotel a little further from the centre then return to their hotel the following day when they would have a room available. Fantastic customer service, and they even organised the taxis to and from the other hotel – all's well that ends well, and all that, but you really don't want to be having that kind of carry-on in a strange city at midnight!

Right, that's enough of playing catch-up. Let's get back to where we left off…

CHAPTER 2

Love is in the air

(2002, revisited!)

OK, this is the special chronological diversion I cunningly hinted at in the last chapter of Volume 2, so events here are starting from the end of the *Grand Tour*...

Going back to work after the summer of 2001 was one thing, but getting down to some serious wedding research was far more important. We felt we'd blown a chance by not achieving much "on the ground" during the summer, so we quickly set about gathering information by writing to the Italian Consulate, collecting wedding "package" brochures from the big travel companies – we knew we didn't want a package, but we reckoned we might glean some useful information – and stepping up what was now becoming more established as standard practice, internet research.

One way or another, it all slowly began to come together. We located a wedding planner in Sorrento, Sandra, that could set everything up locally and guide us through the bureaucratic maze, and this was our great leap forward. Sandra was half English, half Italian and had been brought up and educated half in London, half in Sorrento – thereby speaking both native English and native Italian – result! Over the next few months, we arrived at the decision that we would get married during our Easter holidays, and that we would source a flight-and-hotel package holiday deal in order to simplify the travel and accommodation arrangements. Those had to be simple, as we were to be taking my dad, Angela's parents and Ted (our friend from Edinburgh, who you heard about in Book 2) with us. However, I couldn't escape the feeling that much of it might turn out to be like herding cats, and I was right.

Fiona and Mirek (our friends from Montreal who you also met in Book 2) were joining us too, as were my aunt Rose and her husband David from Toronto. We hadn't actually invited Rose – in fact, we didn't invite anyone apart from our immediate family as we didn't want to make anyone feel obliged to spend all that money on a foreign trip just for us – so Rose invited herself! But we were happy and humbled that she and David, and everyone else, had chosen to share in our special day.

Various documents were despatched to Sandra so she could put everything in place, and eventually we confirmed an early-April date as our big day. We would arrive a week before – by law we had to be in Italy for a full week before the wedding, but that also left us plenty of time for any last-minute, on-the-spot arrangements – then still have a complete week afterwards for our honeymoon, albeit with an army of hangers-on in tow. I jest – we wouldn't have had it any other way. Well, I say that…

Our flights left from Manchester on a Friday, so on the Thursday, my dad drove Angela's parents, Ruth and Eddie, up from Carnoustie to our house, and we transferred everyone's luggage into our two cars before heading to Edinburgh to pick up Ted. Then it was full steam ahead to Manchester – or Stockport to be precise. Or it should've been full steam ahead, but we had to stop at Dreghorn, on the western edge of Edinburgh, for lunch!

We'd only just got going, but here was the first incident of the trip. I'd thought we could stop for lunch somewhere around the border, thus nicely splitting the journey, but was overruled as that would apparently be too late for lunch. At Dreghorn, as we prepared to enter the Little Chef, there appeared to be a bit of hesitation in the ranks, and we discovered that Eddie didn't want to go in there. That left pre-packed sandwiches from the petrol station as the only immediately available option, and so, a full 15 minutes into this next leg of the journey, there we were, sitting in a petrol station car park scoffing sandwiches and giving each other the evil eye.

I had already upset my dad by announcing that I would take most of the luggage in my car with Ted, and that he would travel with Angela, Ruth and Eddie. Logistically, this made sense as the rear seats folded down in my car, thus allowing all the luggage in, but also meant there could be only one front-seat passenger. As Ruth and Eddie had to be together, I didn't think it was fair for Ted to go in that car as he didn't really know them at that stage. Dad did, so the arrangement was obvious really. Still, he wasn't convinced – nothing serious but definitely not happy.

Finally, we were off. I was the lead car, and all the way down, I could see in my mirror that there wasn't much in the way of conversation going on in Angela's car, and I could see my dad's little face staring over the centre console from the back seat, probably wondering about what could've been... Meanwhile, Ted and I were having a great laugh.

When we finally arrived in Stockport, we had to ferry all the luggage into the hotel ready for the taxi next morning, as the cars would stay there while we were away. As an economy measure, we'd decided to book only two rooms with Angela, Ruth and Eddie in one, and the three musketeers in the other. Ruth immediately made herself comfortable in their room, and by the time Angela and her dad struggled in with the luggage, she already had a coffee on the go, for herself, and was fiddling with the TV remote. As they tried manfully, and womanfully, to negotiate the cases round the bed, Ruth demanded that they fix the telly as she couldn't get it to work – magic moments! We had a meal in an Italian restaurant in Stockport that evening, reliving the events of the day and looking forward to the big adventure to come.

The next day started around 6 a.m. for me, though not through choice. Ted's background in both the army and the Royal Mail meant he was always up early, and my dad wasn't a late sleeper either. So the two of them were crashing around from stupid o'clock while I tried heroically to keep on sleeping. Eventually, around 9 a.m., I had to give in and get up so we could all go for breakfast.

The taxi to the airport and check-in were thankfully uneventful, which left plenty of time for our next drama. My dad had been worried about ear wax on the plane – he'd had a ruptured ear drum when he was younger – and when he spotted an NHS walk-in centre in the airport, he decided this was too good an opportunity to pass up. But by the time he'd waited in line and was eventually seen to, we were running a wee bit late, and we all had to rush through passport control to get to our departure gate just in time. Angela was all for killing him, just as I'd been ready to have her dad at Dreghorn. So it was now 1–1, though it would've been pointless trying to keep a score by the end of the fortnight.

We arrived in Naples and the "herding cats" analogy came back into play. As we waited at the baggage carousel, I decided the best way to keep everyone under control was to allocate specific jobs, so I detailed each of them to look out for their own bags, then Ted and I would grab them as they identified them. After we'd reclaimed a couple, we seemed to be waiting for ages, so I looked around to check that Ruth was still paying attention. She wasn't even there! She'd wandered off, so I tracked her down and said, "I thought you were meant to be watching for your bags?" Without missing a beat, she turned to Eddie and angrily said, "Why are you not watching?" Again, priceless.

Eventually, we had all the bags off, except one – the one containing Angela's wedding dress! It did come through, but the fact it was last, and that there was a significant delay before it appeared, did nothing for our nerves.

With both the requisite number of cases and people accounted for, we boarded our bus for what should've been a one-hour journey to Sorrento. The thing was, it was Good Friday – a huge day in the Italian Catholic calendar – and there were great processions going on in each of the towns en route, which resulted in a considerable delay in our progress.

The parade in Sorrento itself was in full swing when we finally arrived, so it provided the biggest delay. So much so that quite a few of the older male passengers, Eddie included, had to make an emergency escape into some waste ground to answer the call of nature. Unfortunately for Eddie, he chose to do it just as the bus was finally about to move off, but he made it back in time – just! When we arrived at our beautiful location, the Grand Hotel de la Ville, we were about three hours later than planned, but thankfully they had held back a dinner service for the late arrivals. Finally, we could relax.

In the morning, refreshed after a good night's sleep and a leisurely breakfast, Angela, me, Dad and Ted strolled into downtown Sorrento together. Primarily, this was to give them their bearings – Ruth and Eddie had been there before, so they were doing their own thing. As it was a Saturday, Ted wanted to check out the local bars to find out if anyone was showing football, especially Scottish football, and Dad was up for that too.

We took them along the main street, Corso Italia, and headed for an English bar, Chaplin's, that we reckoned would be the safest bet. We were standing in the doorway as Ted checked the place out, and just as he returned to say that this would do fine, there was a lot of whooping and screaming on the street behind us – Fiona and Mirek had been walking along Corso Italia from the other direction and had just spotted Angela! This was great as we hadn't been sure how exactly, or when, we were going to hook up – remember, this was before the normalisation of mobile phones! Leaving Dad and Ted in the bar watching football, we struck off into Sorrento to catch up. Happy days indeed.

Later that afternoon, we met Sandra for the first time. She came to the hotel and didn't look anything like we'd imagined, wandering in looking a bit dishevelled and carrying a crash helmet. Anyway, looks can be deceptive, and she was really nice. She reassured us that everything had been organised as previously planned and also detailed the sorts of things we still had to arrange ourselves, leaving us with some choices to make. We arranged to meet up again over the next few days to go and look at some reception venues, florists and so on.

Most of the rest of that week is a blur, sequentially at any rate, so I should just go for the edited highlights. The florist was an easy choice as the first one Sandra took us to was excellent, reasonably priced and said they would locate thistles – *cardi* in Italian – for us to wear as buttonholes. Similarly, it only took a few restaurant and hotel visits to decide that our absolutely ideal venue was the beautiful Palazzo Marziale. This was stunning, and just around the corner from the town hall where our ceremony would take place. Everything had come together perfectly. Fiona was our official photographer, Angela would do her own hair and make-up, and Ted was put in charge of getting her dress prepared before the ceremony as he had already established a rapport with a local dry-cleaner – don't ask! At some point during all this activity, Rose and David had arrived and our merry band was complete. All we had to do now was get married!

Around 5 a.m. on our wedding day, Angela and I were awoken suddenly by a noise we recognised all too well. Looking out of our bedroom window, we were dismayed to see slate-grey skies and typically Scottish rain battering down horizontally – I say dismayed, but Angela was beside herself! "How can it rain? We could get this at home!" and other plaintiff cries emanated from her, wee soul, while I did that typically male thing of gentle reassurance: "It'll be OK. There's plenty time yet..." I'm not sure I believed it myself mind, but I had to think positive.

Now, I know that, in relative terms, a bit of rain on your wedding day isn't up there with the worst that can happen, but it's not so easy to see that when you're totally consumed by your own "moment". We went back to bed but didn't sleep much; we just hoped and prayed that everything would turn out alright. Ever practical, Angela was already making plans for wearing plastic bags over her shoes and thinking of ways to keep her dress clean…

As we went down for breakfast, sharing our gloom with our family, the rain began to subside and finally, around 11 a.m., the sun broke through. By the time the ceremony was due to start, at noon, the sun was brilliant and had burned away all traces of the rain. Phew!

After showering and shaving, I left our room to get dressed along with Dad and Ted, leaving Angela in the care of "the girls" – Ruth, Rose and Fiona… It was probably just as well Fiona was there. Ted had taken my shoes off me as soon as we arrived, declaring that he would "bull" them using his army training. I protested that they were brand new and unworn, but he insisted. When he produced them on the day, I can honestly say I've never seen a better polished pair of shoes! Whatever else soldiers are trained to do, they sure can polish shoes, and, apart from an occasional buff with a cloth, those shoes have remained pristine for coming up on 25 years.

A drama then unfolded between Ted and Dad as Ted produced his kilt outfit. Now, we didn't know that he was bringing it, and we had earlier dissuaded Dad from wearing the kilt due to Eddie's reluctance to wear one. Anyway, tiffs aside, Ted looked good in his kilt, while Dad was carrying off effortless elegance in a smart black suit. I was in the full Highland outfit and felt great. Mirek arrived sporting a classic American tuxedo with the most ridiculous lining I have ever seen – "It was a great deal!" he protested. The *cardo* (thistle) buttonholes completed the look, and we set off for the *municipio* (town hall) in great spirits, thanking the weather gods again for the change in the weather.

As that weather was by now absolutely perfect – beautifully warm with bright sunshine and a clear blue Mediterranean sky – the ceremony was able to take place outside in the town hall courtyard as originally planned. It was simply idyllic. The sight of a couple of guys in kilts certainly caught the attention of the locals, and we attracted a bit of an audience outside the venue.

Then Angela arrived... She looked beautiful, absolutely stunning – which I knew, of course, nothing new there – but this was different. People talk about brides looking radiant, and she certainly did.

The ceremony itself was an entertaining experience, totally conducted in Italian with Sandra translating for us. We all giggled as the mayor stumbled over her pronunciation of my name. Now, at this point it's probably worth explaining that, for official purposes, the Italian norm is to use surname followed by given name, and as they don't really get middle names, they just tag mine on to my given name. For reasons best known to herself, the mayor then chose McIntosh instead of Gordon to precede my surname and addressed me as "McIntosh Craigie". But as she struggled with the harsh Scottish sounds... well, it didn't sound much like it should've done, so Angela always reminds me that she married some guy called "Mickintosh Graige"!

There was also much to giggle about in the translation of the declaration – there's none of this "love, honour and obey" nonsense from the Italians, oh no. Instead, amongst other things, we agreed that "both husband and wife have a duty, each according to his or her own possessions and professional or domestic skills, to contribute towards the needs of the family". Angela still asks me on a regular basis what exactly my skills are – harsh!

Then it was time for signatures, and there seemed to be quite a few of those. I can still hear clearly one of my dad's daftisms: "You can't say it's not real now, Gordon, after all those signatures!" Bless.

All the while, Fiona was taking photographs, then we went outside to have the traditional sugared almonds thrown at us – Ruth nearly took my eye out, deliberately I'm sure, as retribution for taking away her daughter! A big crowd saw us off on our traditional horse and carriage procession around Sorrento, locals smiling and calling out *auguri* – congratulations – as we passed.

Around 20 minutes later, we arrived back at Palazzo Marziale blissfully happy and completely unaware of the drama that had apparently happened in our absence. Now, from the town hall to the palazzo is approximately 10 metres around a corner. Someone – the culprit has never confessed – in the assembled company had decided that they knew exactly where it was and promptly escorted our entire entourage off to a completely different location!

Anyway, eventually they'd somehow managed to sort themselves out and were all present and correctly in place by the time we showed up. Directly across the road from Palazzo Marziale is the 14th-century Francescan Cloisters, and we went in there first to take some more photographs before entering the palazzo. The first part of our celebrations was to be *prosecchi* all round on the balcony, so I got to show off – seriously – my legendary champagne/Prosecco bottle opening skills by expertly removing the cork without mess, and we all toasted our marriage.

As we mingled and chatted, Fiona was still posing Angela and me – mainly Angela! – for more photographs. One pose involved Angela sitting on the wall so as to get a great shot with the Bay of Naples in the background. On the other side of the wall was a sheer drop to the street, about four metres below, and this caused Eddie's fatherly anxiety levels to go through the roof. "Angie, Angie, be careful," he barked, almost scaring her into falling. Great memories.

The meal was exquisite, and I've always regretted not properly preparing my speech. I did manage to say something about how a princess deserved to be married in a palazzo, and it did seem to go down well as it was all heartfelt, but I could've and should've said so much more. Mind you, with the heckling I was getting, especially from my new bride, I'm amazed I got through anything.

After the beautiful meal and more chit-chat on the terrace, Angela and I left with Fiona and Mirek to take some more photographs around Sorrento. We had the use of the palazzo for as long as we wanted, infinite drinks, coffees and so on included, so we left the oldies to rest and soak up the luxurious surroundings until we returned. We took umpteen photos in the many lovely spots on the way down to the harbour before returning an hour or so later.

Just as we arrived back, we were perplexed to see Ruth and Rose getting in a taxi to go back to the hotel. We'd been hoping to spend some more time at the palazzo, but our elders had decided that the party was over because we'd abandoned them, and they were aff! Feeling more than a little peeved, we decided that we should adjourn to our favourite Sorrento bar, Bar Vittoria, just across the road and that, while the girls would go back to base and change, the boys would start the festivities right away. Fiona and Mirek were staying just round the corner, so they quickly got into their casual clothes leaving me and Ted a little exposed in our kilts, but what the hell!

Anyway, a great evening was had by all, and we finally called it a night approaching midnight. Again, the girls got a taxi back, but us hardy lads set off on foot, the locals resplendent in their winter coats and puffa jackets – Italians do not consider early April to be short-sleeve weather! – while Ted and I marched down the middle of Corso Italia in our kilts, much to their amazement and amusement! Fantastic memories.

Let's have a quick run through some of the edited highlights, or out-takes, from our two weeks in Sorrento.

There was an older woman holidaying in our hotel on her own, and Ruth got into conversation with her, after our first night's dinner, when she went through to the bar area for a cigarette and a coffee while the rest of us stayed in the dining room. We'd already noticed this woman sitting nearby as she was making light work of a bottle of red – we very quickly, and somewhat uncharitably, nicknamed her Maisie Lush.

Anyway, the two of them got on like a house on fire and were always blethering away conspiratorially. Maisie liked her *vinho tinto* – as she insisted on calling it even though that's actually Portuguese for "red wine"! – and they'd already told each other their life stories by the time we joined them...

just in time to hear Ruth recall a dream she'd had about her children that she reckoned had come true. Apparently, she'd once dreamed that all four kids were grown up and wearing white coats, and that had come to pass since Angela, Edward and Sally were all scientists, and young Ruth was... a cook! And, unlike Maisie, old Ruth was teetotal so nae drink was involved in the spinning of this yarn.

As everybody else was coupled up, Ted and Dad tended to go around together when we weren't engaged in group activities. Ted, however, did make the occasional bid for freedom to have some time on his own, and witnessing my dad's attempts to track him down caused us great hilarity. There was one evening when Dad did about three laps of Sorrento trying to find Ted while we all knew he was in the hotel lounge bar watching football.

One of Ted's other secret hidey-holes was a small bar just around the corner which was run by a husband-and-wife team. The woman did, however, look somewhat androgynous – a look exacerbated by the standard white shirt/black tie waiter uniform – so Ted wasn't entirely sure if she was a woman or not. After a few visits, the couple had clearly recognised him and kind of adopted him as a regular, so the woman leaned over the bar and said – or rather, what Ted heard was – "Do you wanna dry keks?" The way Ted told us this story, I can completely see the look he must've had on his face!

Realising that he didn't understand, she said it again: "Do you wanna dry keks?" Ted was clearly uneasy as, by now, the husband was taking an interest in the exchange and came across to help. After reaching under the bar, he produced a plate of cakes and pushed them encouragingly towards

Ted, who belatedly realised the question was, "Do you want to try cakes?" This came as a mighty relief to our poor Edinburgh loon as, in his dialect, keks are underpants, and he was beginning to panic at the thought of his androgynous host enquiring about the dry state of his, or her, underwear!

The day after the ceremony, Angela felt unwell – a bit sick and generally not right – and we decided she should probably stay in bed until whatever was affecting her had passed. The hotel staff were kind enough to deliver breakfast and dinner up to our room, not that Angela ate much of it, but it meant I could stay with her. Her mum was happy to tell anyone who was willing to listen that it was down to all the excitement of the previous day, despite the fact that it was clearly more likely to be mild food poisoning or a wee bug she'd picked up. Anyway, that wasn't quite as off the wall as what greeted us the following day when we went down for breakfast, with Angela fully recovered, as the head waiter took me aside and shook me by the hand, whispering, "Fast work, my friend!" Aye, and it wisnae morning sickness either…

There are many other stories from that trip, and I could probably write an entire book about it, in truth. But I'll confine myself to just one more – the team outing to Capri. Angela and I had been before, but we reckoned that the best way to ensure everybody could see the island safely and reasonably was for us to escort them – talk about taking one for the team! On the boat, we were approached by a tout offering chauffeured tours around the island which, me being naturally suspicious of anything organised, we rebuffed. This led to our first marital disagreement. Angela started to think that maybe it was a good idea, and Ruth and Rose seemed quite keen, but I maintained it was a scam, a rip-off, and we should have nothing to do with it.

We arrived on Capri, herded everyone onto the funicular and arrived safely in the town centre. Pointing out the various directions everyone could go in, we waved them off and set off on our own. Immediately, Angela was on at me about abandoning them and how the tour would've been good for them. I protested that we needed time alone and that they were all very capable of getting around the main parts of Capri independently.

Just then we came across Ruth, Eddie, Rose and David sitting having coffee in a bar already, and they said Dad and Ted had just passed.

Moving on, Angela started on me again, and this time, none too graciously I must admit, I said, "Fine, whatever, let's check it out." We approached a taxi driver, Carlos, and agreed a deal for him and his mate to take us around in two cars. Then all we had to do was herd up the oldies, so we went back to the bar, and their wee faces fair lit up when we told them what we'd arranged. We soon found the Dynamic Duo not too far away as well. Carlos decided he would take "the girls" plus me, as it was my honeymoon. That meant the four boys were in the other car with a younger driver.

Carlos was a character. He'd actually been featured once in the *Daily Record* as "Charlie the singing taxi driver", and he was a bit of a legend. He didnae half put on the patter, and the girls lapped it up, especially Ruth and Rose! It turned out to be a great idea and a fabulous day, and so, not for the first or last time, Angela was right – well done, babe!

About halfway round, we went up a cable car to reach the highest point of the island, and it was quite exciting and nerve-wracking making sure everyone got on and off alright – the cable car was in continuous motion which meant we had to catch our elderly companions as they disembarked.

Then we visited the Blue Grotto, always a spectacular sight. Again, we knew what to expect from a previous visit, but we had to warn everyone to be careful as the waves can throw you against the rocks at the narrow entrance. In the boys' boat, either Eddie or David hit their head on the rocks, and in our boat, I got a skinned elbow trying to force the boat down so the girls' heads stayed out of the danger zone. Any slight pain was well worth it for the spectacle and the memory. At various points, Carlos was justifying his singing reputation by serenading the ladies, and he really did have them eating out of the palm of his hand.

As we were nearing the finish, he pulled the car over and said, "Listen, if you want to give me a tip, you should give me it now. If you wait until the end, then the other driver will see, and he'll want a tip too, but he won't have been singing or entertaining. But only if you want to."

Hook, line, sinker! Ruth and Rose were right into that: "Oh yes, Carlos, of course, Carlos, how much would you like, Carlos." So we cobbled together a sizeable tip and headed back to the town with a very happy Carlos.

When the car drew up, Rose ran off towards David to stop him from tipping the other guy but, too late, as he'd pulled a similar scam! Ach well, it wasn't that much, and in hindsight it was a priceless experience anyway. But it does go to show how gullible women can be... Sorry, Angela!

Then, all too quickly, the holiday/wedding/honeymoon was over, and we had to be up at the crack of dawn to board the coach back to Naples Airport. That wasn't the end of the fun and games though, oh no, not by a long shot. As is the custom in some hotels, all the drinks and coffees and whatever during your stay are charged to your room number for settlement at the end of your stay. It's probably either to avoid the staff fiddling the cash or, less cynically, to simplify cash-handling, but, whatever, you're presented with your account as you're checking out.

So, at around 6 a.m., as we were sleepily filing in for a quick breakfast before leaving, we picked up the bills at reception. They all seemed reasonable – we'd taken turns buying the wine at dinner each night, and there were a few drinks and coffees here and there for everyone – so we each quickly settled up and boarded the coach. As we were driving through a sleepy and slightly misty Sorrento, we became aware that Eddie was fretting over his bill. This wasn't too much of a surprise as Eddie fretted over most things, but on closer inspection, his bill did seem a good bit longer than everyone else's. In fact, as the sheets unfolded, he looked a bit like the Andrex puppy, his bill was that long.

Anyway, he was convinced he'd been diddled, but when we looked more closely at the detail, we could see there were multiple charges of exactly the same amount. And, as they were timed, we could see that most of them had been charged between around 11 p.m. and 3 a.m. every day. Proof that he'd been done? No, proof that Ruth had been drinking copious amounts of coffee in the bar every night when she couldn't sleep – and probably why she couldn't sleep, come to think of it!

She'd been telling us every day that she'd been down in the bar the night before chatting to Gino when she couldn't sleep. "Oh, Gino's awfy nice," she kept telling us. "We have a laugh, and he just gives me my coffees, and I tell him to have one too." Well, every time Gino "gave" her a coffee, he rang it up along with the one he was having (or pocketing?) too, and that's why Eddie's bill was huge. We used to cast that story up to Ruth afterwards, and we always had a good laugh over it, especially her. I'm not entirely sure Eddie ever quite got the funny side of it though…

By the time we rolled into Capodichino Airport in Naples, the mist had cleared and we were into another gloriously sunny Mediterranean day, just as we were heading home. As a very small, ex-military airport, Capodichino wasn't exactly luxuriously appointed, and once we'd passed through security, we were in what was essentially a medium-sized waiting room with no duty-free shopping opportunities. Dad had wanted to buy cigarettes to take home for his brother, Andy, and had planned to buy them duty-free. Ruth told him he could go back through security and buy them in the airport as they would still be cheaper than back home anyway, and that's what she'd done. So Ted and I accompanied him back to the security gate and gave him strict instructions as to what to do and, importantly, not to be too long.

After standing around waiting for a few minutes, Ted told me to go back and he'd keep an eye out for Dad. About 15 minutes later, the two of them returned with yet another tale to tell. Dad's command of Italian wasn't great (!) and when he was allowed to go back into the airport, he'd thought the security guy had told him to just come through this side channel when he returned.

Ted watched the scene unfold – as Dad returned he ignored the security queues and breezed up this side channel, smiling at the security personnel behind the glass and pointing at his carrier bag, saying, "It's just me – I've got them," and carrying on his merry way. Cue all manner of panic as security men rushed around, shouting and drawing their pistols, while Ted shouted to my dad, "Tam, Tam, you've got to go through the gates!"

As well as not being fluent in Italian, Dad wasn't 100 per cent in the hearing department either, so he simply carried on, smiling away at all and sundry. Eventually, he was stopped and, despite one or two angry exchanges, one of the security men eventually took pity on him and escorted him back through the proper way before allowing him to rejoin Ted on the other side. He still didn't think he'd done anything wrong!

Anyway, replete with cigarettes and having escaped being shot, a prison sentence or both, his and our Italian adventure was over, and we returned home without further incident. Back home and back to work, but still we had more important stuff to concentrate on as another momentous event was only about a month away...

... when we gathered around 120 friends and family at the Dundee Hilton Hotel for our wedding reception in the middle of May. Angela had the somewhat unusual pleasure of wearing her wedding dress again, thus ensuring full value for money, and I was once again fully kilted. In fact, most of the principal players – Angela, me, Ruth, Eddie and Ted all looked exactly the same as we had in Sorrento, but Dad took the opportunity to make amends and wear his kilt – well, his brother Andy's kilt, to be precise – and absolutely splendid he looked too!

We both have so many happy memories of that evening, obviously, and some of the finest concern my dad. While he was holding court, in full Highland dress with all his family around him, he was absolutely in his element. Angela and I still laugh when we recall a vision we both share of him prowling – the only word for it – across the dance floor with his arm outstretched, pointing in the direction of his identified "victim", or dance partner, before strutting his stuff in his kilt.

His other personal proud moment that night came when we unveiled the wedding cake – a beautiful three-tier vision created entirely by Dad's fair hand. He had a little help from my cousin David, a trained pastry chef, with the icing, but it was entirely his own work. We'd described something simple and clean – often the hardest to pull off! – and he'd produced it to perfection, the icing seemingly draped over the tiers like folded sheets. And it tasted good too.

We put a lot of effort into the planning of the event, including tweaking the buffet menu on offer and negotiating our own concoctions into the deal. The result was stunning apparently. I say apparently as neither of us actually ate any of the food – it was so good that it was all gone before we got to it! Ach well, at least our guests enjoyed it, and several took the trouble to tell us how good it was and how they'd gone back for seconds – and thirds.

We also selected some of the music carefully. I would've scripted the entire set if I'd had the time, but I was overruled by both Angela and the DJ. However, we made sure some key tunes were played. We performed our first dance to "More Than Words" by Extreme before getting the party absolutely started with the Dave Edmunds classic "I Knew the Bride (When She Used to Rock and Roll)". Later, we restarted the dancing after the buffet break with Sweet's

"The Ballroom Blitz" followed by "Love Is in the Air" by John Paul Young – famously a Dundee United anthem – for which Angela dragged our Dundee-supporting friend Dougie onto the floor knowing that he couldn't refuse the bride! Great stuff.

So many memories from just one night, but just one wee story to finish it off. Part of the deal with the hotel was that we had a room to change in beforehand and stay in overnight. What they hadn't told us was that they'd allocated us the bridal suite, with stunning views over the Tay. We turned up around 6 p.m. on the Saturday night to discover that we could've been lounging in this luxury and enjoying all the hotel facilities all afternoon! Instead, we only had half an hour over a coffee before getting ready to greet our guests, returning to the room around 3 a.m. elated but shattered, then up around 10 a.m. with just enough time to shower and pack up before the party was well and truly over. Rats!

Well, not quite over, as we'd invited anyone who was still around to join us back at our house for brunch. Around 20-odd folks made it up for bacon rolls and suchlike, and it was a great way to round off a fantastic weekend. Happy memories again.

Sticking with the theme – though not the chronology as we're fast-forwarding several months here – my dad's final contribution to our wedding was to gather the video footage from Eddie's camera and produce an edited programme complete with music. We had no idea he was doing this, but with the help of a friend, a video production professional, he produced an extremely polished effort.

Later, he revisited the project and digitised the whole thing, so we have a DVD record of both the wedding and reception. This wasn't easy for him, particularly as it transpired that some of the footage from Sorrento had been recorded over. Apparently, Eddie had been looking through it and forgot to either fast-forward or remove the tape of the wedding before coming to the reception. On the night, at some point he, or more likely Ruth, had asked their grandson to go round and video the guests. Thankfully, he did the job like any stereotypical teenager and only put minimal effort into it, thereby not filming over too much of the original wedding footage – and, even more thankfully, he'd stopped recording before scrubbing the wedding ceremony itself.

On the downside, we did lose some precious stuff that I've consequently never seen, including Angela sweeping down the stairs of the Grand Hotel de la Ville with her dad and into the taxi with her dress flowing behind her – I would've loved to have seen that. But it could've been so much worse, and the DVD is a great memory of a wonderful day and another fine achievement for my late-developer, silver-surfer father. Thanks, Dad.

[2025 update: In the years since we got married, as weddings abroad have gained in popularity, we've read several useful pieces of advice about what to do and, more importantly, what not to do. One particularly convincing, and common, piece of guidance is for the happy couple never to stay in the same hotel as their guests… Now they tell us! Ach well, think of all the fun we would've missed out on – apart from having my mum and brother with us, I wouldn't change a thing.]

CHAPTER 3

Work to live, or live to work?

(2002–2006)

At the end of Volume 2 – after the not-so-wee tease about the wedding – you'll recall that I was about to leave my secondment at Learning and Teaching Scotland, not to return to Lauder College but to start a new job with a software development company in Edinburgh.

Well, this was all a wee bit different then. I'd stepped out of the sanctity – and, as we shall see, (relative) sanity – of the public sector for the first time, and although exciting, this was also quite scary. In fact, for the first month or so, I'd never been so unhappy because of work. I didn't know what I was doing – literally – and therefore felt totally out of my depth. I know, and even then I knew, that this could easily be rationalised, that everybody feels like this when they change jobs because the whole thing is up there with bereavement and divorce as major life stresses.

But, as it turned out, this feeling ran deeper, though it did take a while to figure that out. In the build-up, when

I was being courted, and headhunted, by the directors, the company was painted as a relaxed, modern, innovative organisation for whom the sky really was the limit. The reality was that one director in particular was a Walter Mitty character and that they'd just lucked out on a couple of big contracts in their start-up period – one of which had been commissioned by me at LTS!

And far from only *feeling* that I didn't know what my job was due to the nerves associated with starting something new, I really didn't know *what* my job was and never quite figured it out over the next year and a half. There was actually a very simple explanation for that – nobody at the company seemed to know either! Eventually, I think they just kind of lost interest in the whole educational side of things and started focusing more on the financial services industry, which they thought they had more insight into. In a moment, we'll see where that ended up. When I was summoned to a meeting one day, it was put to me that the company was going to concentrate on that more in the future. Unsurprisingly, I felt there was no longer a role for me within that context and therefore it was an easy decision to leave. That was in May 2004, and the company went bust three months later… Karma truly is a bitch!

As it turned out, they had no more insight into financial services than they had into education, and their luck had eventually run out. So I'd managed to escape just in time, bruised by the experience certainly but also somehow released from the inevitability of simply climbing, or clinging on to, the educational ladder that had previously been my career path. But not, it seemed, without one more roll of the dice…

When an opportunity arose almost immediately to apply for a job with Her Majesty's Inspectorate of Education

(HMIE), it suddenly seemed like everything that I'd previously done had led to this chance. Putting together my CV and matching my skills and experience to the requirements of the job, well, I was a perfect match, even if I do say so myself.

As a backup, in the unlikely event of them not snapping my hand off, I'd lined up some freelance consultancy work and everything was in place for that to kick off when we returned from our summer holiday, Either way, the future was looking good. The official letter duly arrived from HMIE inviting me to their assessment centre for interview – not many people even get this far – but when I checked the date of the interview... it was two days after we were due to fly out on holiday.

I phoned and asked if it could be postponed, but the answer was, predictably and bureaucratically, no. Some friends and colleagues advised me to change our holiday dates, but I stuck to my principles of prioritising personal and family life above everything else and simply thought, *que sera sera*. I really did believe, however, that the chance would come again in time.

It didn't.

But first, setting all that aside, it was holiday time again, and we jetted off to visit Fiona and Mirek once more in Montreal. This was to be our third visit to their house in the serene suburb of Beaconsfield and, though none of us realised it at the time, our last. The plan was that we would stay in Beaconsfield for a week before driving down together to New York City for five days, then return to Montreal for another couple of weeks.

That first week coincided with the Euro 2004 football championships, and, celebrating Mirek's Czech roots, we visited a local bar to watch his boys take on Greece in the semi-final. Unfortunately, and totally unexpectedly, the Greeks scraped a win and went on, equally unexpectedly, to win the tournament. It was disappointing for us as Mirek, though generally not too fussed about anything Czech – except beer! – had been looking forward to getting together with his dad for the final. Still, the Czechs got closer to glory than Scotland ever do.

The trip to New York was an obvious highlight for Angela and I as neither of us had been before. Mirek reckoned it was around a six-hour drive, but due to weather and traffic, it actually took us closer to 10 hours. Although that was a little gruelling, we didn't want to waste any time when we arrived in the Big Apple, and after a quick turnaround at our accommodation, we all set off in search of the New York City experience. Our rented apartment was on Broadway, quite close to Central Park, so we knew that if we simply walked down Broadway, we'd eventually come to something interesting. And we did.

It was around 10.30 p.m. when we wandered into Times Square, and as we looked around us in wonder at all the huge buildings, illuminated signs and stereotypical New York City views, someone tapped Angela on the shoulder. "What are you doing here?" It was only one of her colleagues from Perth College! What are the chances?

Over the next few days, we did all the touristy things you'd expect, but I suppose my personal highlights, given my love of all things Beatles, were seeing both the Dakota Building, where John Lennon lived and, tragically, died, and his Strawberry Fields Memorial Garden in Central Park, although tinged with a sadness like you experience when visiting the World War I or II battlefields, or Culloden Moor, or other sites where tragedies have occurred. I suppose the reason we all do things like that is a form of honouring memories. At least that's how I like to think about it.

We had a couple of unusual adventures while we were there – nothing too spectacular but enough to keep us all amused whenever we reminisce over that trip.

One evening, as we were getting the subway back to our apartment, I was the last to go through the barrier, but my ticket just wouldn't be accepted. With the others on the platform and the train coming into the station, I did my best Starsky and Hutch impersonation and vaulted the barrier. Thankfully, this was before the omnipresence of CCTV, but, more interestingly, none of the locals batted an eyelid – they were clearly accustomed to this type of behaviour.

Another evening – and I have less justification for this one – we were in a restaurant in Little Italy and had experienced unusually bad service. After having our complaints rudely dismissed, and after reluctantly paying the ridiculous bill, I decided to visit the toilet before leaving. I noticed a few giant containers of liquid soap stored next to the sink and inexplicably decided, on the spur of the moment, that this was my chance for retribution against the shoddy treatment I felt we'd had. Totally out of character – honest! – I poured the soap containers down the sink and into the toilet cistern before returning to the others and declaring, in a hurried tone, "Right, let's get going then."

They were initially confused at my haste, but when I quickly explained why we should leave immediately, we were all in stitches at the prospect of the restaurant's facilities beginning to foam uncontrollably over the rest of the evening. Outside the restaurant, we immediately jumped in a taxi for two reasons – one, to experience a New York yellow taxi ride, and two, to get as much distance as possible between us and the foaming restaurant, pronto. Not big, not clever, deeply sorry… sort of.

It was soon time to head back up to Canada, where we continued to enjoy the North American sunshine, combining the relaxed metropolitan lifestyle of Beaconsfield with the big-city excitement of downtown Montreal for another couple of weeks before returning to Scotland and my new adventure of self-employment.

Before leaving on holiday, I'd been contracted to oversee a technology project for an educational consortium in Lanarkshire, so that was to be my introduction to the freelance lifestyle. From the outset, everything went well, and other projects were rolling in at an extremely healthy, and lucrative, rate. So much so that a couple of months later, I was advised by my accountant – now there's a relationship I'd never envisaged I'd have! – that I should form a limited company instead of operating as a sole trader, and hence, in December 2004, The McIntosh Partnership Limited came into being.

Utilising my mum's maiden name was intended to honour her memory, but this respectful act somewhat backfired when Dad asked me one day if I hadn't used "Craigie" because I didn't like my – his – name! Angela and I had agonised over a company name for ages before coming up with this one too. Our thinking at the time was to keep both our surnames out of it, a bit like ticking the "no publicity" box on the pools' coupon, and The McIntosh Partnership had a prestigious ring to it, or so we thought.

Anyway, notwithstanding this new administrative arrangement, things continued pretty much as before and, to coin a cliché, business was booming. Apart from the ongoing project in Lanarkshire, I managed to get a succession of commissions from Learndirect Scotland – mainly project management gigs related to using technology to enhance learning processes – and established a really good relationship with the people there.

Interestingly, just as things were really kicking into gear, I received an email from a recruitment consultant who'd been asked to sound me out for a role within a different consortium. I arranged to meet the guy at a hotel on the outskirts of Dundee – the whole thing seemed very cloak and dagger! – and he laid out his proposal. Basically, they wanted me to do exactly what I'd been doing for the Edinburgh company, to be a sort of "middleman" bridging the divide between education and technology. It was flattering to be headhunted again, but, after admittedly not too much reflection, I decided to turn down their generous offer, mainly on the basis of "once bitten, twice shy" – my experience with the previous headhunters was still all too fresh in my mind, and I was perfectly at ease with where my head was currently at, thank you very much.

In fact, the business was going so well that by early 2006, I'd decided to scale back on searching for new projects a little in order to study for an updated qualification. It had always been in the back of my mind that everything I either knew or believed about learning in general – and open, flexible and distance learning in particular – was pretty much self-taught and based on my own personal experience. Consequently, I'd always felt slightly insecure about this, and so I wanted to either validate what I thought I knew or actually learn the truth, to give a theoretical underpinning to my practical experience.

And so I embarked on an MSc at the University of Stirling, mixing elements from their Lifelong Learning and Technology Enhanced Learning courses. My thinking was that what I really wanted was to graduate with an MSc in Technology Enhanced Lifelong Learning, but, university regulations being what they are, I was going to have to decide on one or the other titles eventually.

After a few years of straddling the divide, in the summer of 2010, decision time was finally approaching and I was still swithering between the two – you may remember from previous experience how bad I am with choices!

Eventually, my mind was made up when an acquaintance opined that a degree in Lifelong Learning sounded like something you'd get from the Scouts – or Blue Peter. Not the most scientific of justifications, but that swung me towards Technology Enhanced Learning, and I duly graduated with my MSc TEL in November 2010. I say graduated, but I didn't do the cap and gown bit, electing to graduate *in absentia* as Angela had done with her MEd a year previously. Perhaps I should've done the ceremonial bit for my dad's sake? He was so chuffed and insisted on reading my dissertation, about which he concluded, "Contains too many big words, son." Bless.

Rewind to 2006 – that "scaling back" seemed like a good idea at the time and, in common with most of my big decisions, was based on the best information available. What I wasn't to know was what the "what happened next" round was going to visit upon us. Around November, it was announced that the next Holyrood election would be held on 3 May 2007. My immediate reaction was, "Great, there's a real chance that the SNP might win this time." What I hadn't considered was the effect that this election was to have on my freelance opportunities. As soon as the election date was announced, all the organisations that I'd been gaining contracts from basically shut up shop, the official line being, "Well, there may be a change of government, so we can't commit to any projects just now until we know for certain what our future priorities are."

Fair enough, you may say, and only a few months to wait anyway. However, the government did indeed change, and as soon as it did, the mantra became, "The new government is deciding what it wants us to do, and we can't commit to any projects until they've told us." The Scottish Government had embarked on a 100-day period of analysing the current performance of the organisations they'd inherited and figuring out if they were "fit for purpose" and so another three-month delay ensued.

Once this time passed, several of the organisations I'd previously been successful with were merged, others had their remits changed, and they all embarked on a prolonged spell of "navel-gazing" where their priorities turned to internal restructuring before getting on with their new remits. In best quasi-governmental tradition, this took over a year, during which time they weren't looking to outsource any work at all, and, indeed, external consultants had suddenly become decidedly unwelcome as they decided to concentrate the work in-house... This whole self-employment lark was suddenly looking not as easy as it had originally seemed.

Not to worry, diversification was the new game in town, and I picked up a couple of smaller gigs that appeared destined to grow bigger until internal politics killed them off too. By this time, the "scaled back" 2006 had moved through the "deathly quiet" 2007 into the "hopeful signs" of 2008 then into the "here we go again" desperation of 2009. Once again, just when they thought it was all over, one of my marketing approaches paid off and, courtesy of an old friend and colleague, I picked up a good college-based project that was to see us through the next two years at a reasonable level.

Then, in 2011, we got the double whammy of the fantastic and historic SNP landslide victory at the election. I say "double whammy" because on the one hand, this was fantastic news for me and my political beliefs – and, more importantly, for Scotland! – but, on the other hand, the restrictions imposed on them by the UK Government resulted in the biggest cutbacks in college funding ever seen. This was definitely bad news for external consultants...

Meanwhile – rewinding to 2005 – Fiona and Mirek had decided to take the plunge and head off to the not-so-wild west as Mirek's job was being transferred to Texas. Any doubts they may have had over this move were apparently dispelled when Mirek discovered that it was against the Texas constitution to levy income tax... sorry, Mirko! But seriously, swapping the cold winters of Montreal for the heat of Texas – and no income tax! – held enough appeal for our intrepid friends to up sticks and relocate to the small city of Keller in the Dallas–Fort Worth metroplex.

While they were settling in over the "winter" of 2005/06 – and sending us photos of them cycling wearing shorts and T-shirts on Christmas Day while we were literally shivering in the snow! – a plan was taking shape for us to visit their new abode during our Easter holiday. This was to prove memorable for more than a few reasons...

For starters, this trip included the longest flight we'd ever undertaken as the London to Dallas part was around 10 hours, and we'd actually been on the move for around 13 or 14 hours in total by the time Fiona and Mirek picked us up at Dallas Fort Worth Airport and ferried us "home" to Keller. The upshot of that long day was that after eating, drinking and catching up, at around 11 p.m. I just crashed and burned, literally falling asleep in the middle of a sentence and only waking up because the others were laughing so loudly.

Next morning though, we had to be up bright and early as Fiona had a 10k race starting at 9 a.m. – it was disconcertingly dark when we got up, but we were adequately refreshed and eager to see what downtown Dallas had to offer.

Fiona's run started and ended at the Cotton Bowl, the famous old stadium where Dundee United had played as Dallas Tornado in the inaugural North American Soccer League back in 1967 – who would've guessed there'd be a United connection, eh? So for that reason alone, I was happy to wander around admiring the impressive art deco façade while Fiona went through her pre-race formalities.

We waited to cheer her off before going to partake in Mirek's ritual on race days – breakfast! He has a range of places he likes to visit to while away the hour or so before she's collected her inevitable prize – she's that good – though, if memory serves me correctly, around the Cotton Bowl wasn't an area overly blessed with breakfast joints, so we ended up in a McDonald's. Not the best choice for a vegetarian, but I managed to find something while Angela and Mirek demolished the traditional Maccy D's breakfast offering.

After the race, we spotted a sports shop across the road from the stadium, and I thought it would be the obvious place to locate a retro Dallas Tornado football top – it was the experience of playing in tangerine as the Tornados that convinced then United manager Jerry Kerr (at his wife's suggestion!) to modernise United's colours. She'd observed that plenty of clubs used black-and-white kit, but she didn't know of any playing in tangerine, certainly not in Scotland. The Dallas Tornado kit was tangerine with light blue trim, but, reasoning correctly that no self-respecting Dundee United fan would want any shade of blue in their team colours, Jerry decided that tangerine and black would do the job, and that's why United's official colours were changed a couple of years later. The history you learn reading this book...

Anyway, I asked one of the young assistants if they had any retro tops from 1967 and, after initially looking a bit bemused, she said, "I don't think so, but wait a minute, I'll ask the owner – he played for the Tornados back in the day."

The owner duly arrived and listened with interest to my tale before saying, "No, sorry, we've never had anything like that, but, gee, I'd buy one of those!"

Apart from my disappointment at not being able to find a top, I was also a little taken aback by his response from a business point of view – "gee, I'd buy one of those" – he owned a sports shop! George W. Bush is once alleged to have criticised French business innovation by stating that, "The French don't even have a word for *entrepreneur*" – so Trump clearly isn't the first idiot to occupy the White House! – but this shop owner was proving that average Americans aren't all that savvy either...

We visited many interesting places, including Grapevine, a small town with a main street that's been recreated to look like something from the cowboy days with wooden walkways linking the shops, bars and restaurants. We went into one store selling high-end coffee machines, and while I was looking enviously at a beautiful Jura machine, the owner came over and asked if we'd like to try it. I immediately recognised his accent as being from Stoke – I'd spent a wee bit of time there, you may recall? – so I asked him if he was a Potter or a Valiant? He looked a wee bit surprised but quickly declared his hatred of Stoke City and his love for Port Vale. He also had some connection with the club – maybe his brother was on the board, I don't remember exactly, and that he'd met another board member a few times: Robbie Williams!

Good relations well and truly established, he proceeded to demonstrate the machine and how flexible the settings were, offering two or three coffees each as he altered the settings. Each variation was good, but the last was special, so much so that I was sorely tempted to hand him the $1,000 price there and then. Resisting the temptation on the basis that we'd never be able to transport it home on the plane, we said our farewells and returned to the street.

Another interesting shop we came across had a variety of quirky, arty, household items. Angela was particularly keen on a stained-glass window frame and, after a remarkable piece of talking up by the owner, and haggling on the price, we became the proud owners of a stained-glass window which, apparently, was going to be much easier to take home on a plane than a super-duper coffee machine. We'll see how that turned out later…

We also took a trip out to the sexily-named Pizza Hut Park to see a football – sorry, "sakker" – match between FC Dallas and Chicago Fire. It was the first game of what turned out to be a very successful season for Dallas at their new stadium in Frisco, a 45-minute drive away from Keller. The game itself, which ended in a 3–2 victory for Dallas, was fairly unremarkable except for two things. A guy sitting in front of us with his young son only got animated about the game when he started screaming at the referee, "Yellow card, yellow card," after what seemed to me to be an innocuous foul, then cheering wildly when the ref obliged. Crazy. The other thing was that when we'd just entered the stadium and were scanning the horizon, taking it all in, the very first thing I spotted was a guy wearing a Dundee United top at the far end of the ground – us Arabs get everywhere!

Our fortnight in Texas also included a visit to the famous Southfork Ranch of the 1970s/80s soap opera *Dallas*. The most interesting thing about that was that the swimming pool in the garden – where the bemuscled Bobby ploughed up and down before breakfast, and the bikinied babes Lucy, Pam and the evil Sue Ellen, topped up their tans and/or downed their cocktails – was absolutely tiny! Apparently, they just used clever camera angles to enhance its scale and, for Bobby's swimathons, employed a wave machine so that it looked like he was moving forward when he was actually swimming "on the spot". Who said the camera never lies?

On our "last" evening – the reason for the quotes there will become clear soon enough! – we headed out for a real cowboy cultural carry-on by visiting the famous Billy Bob's Texas, which claims to be the "world's largest honky tonk", whatever that actually means. This place is famous worldwide for its celebration of country music and dancing, as well as a range of other cowboy-centric events. As we all entered, ready and willing to "hoedown for the showdown", it was immediately apparent that we stuck out a wee bit like sore thumbs dress-wise, although Mirek would claim that his belt buckle allowed him to fit in. It didnae.

Neither Mirko nor myself are what you would call "enthusiastic" dancers, especially with the synchronised group line dancing that was very much the evening's speciality, but Angela and Fiona were right into it, gien it laldy while us boring boys embraced more of a spectator role. Ironically, having developed a wee interest in some forms of country music in recent years, particularly the more contemporary country rock, I would probably enjoy the experience more now than I did then... though I'm still no sure aboot the line dancing!

The next day, after breakfast, we were busy packing everything up and making sure we hadn't left anything behind, like the odd stained-glass window or something like that, and had everything well organised to get dropped off at the airport after lunch in plenty of time for our late-afternoon flight. While I was tidying up the last few bits and pieces, Angela was outside helping Mirek put some rubbish in their bins. The last thing I had to do was to check we definitely had our passports and tickets. I looked at the ticket and immediately thought there was something not quite right with the date, so I pulled out my Palm Organiser – an extremely yuppy, upmarket digital diary, very much of its time! – to check the date... I double-checked again then headed outside, crestfallen, to find a giggling Angela and Mirek returning from their bin duties.

"What's up with you?" Angela asked.

"You're never going to believe this, but... our flight was yesterday!"

They both laughed, and Angela replied, "Yeah, good try!" and carried on laughing.

"No, I'm not joking – our flight was yesterday." And I showed her our tickets.

We, or most probably I – Angela will certainly say that! – had made the classic mistake involving overnight flights and had confused our arrival date with our departure date. The flight was, indeed, yesterday...

Panic ensued. We phoned British Airways and told them the tale and were offered seats on today's flight... at around

$1,000 each! Meanwhile, Fiona was searching the internet and came up with Lufthansa flights at $600 each, which was obviously a better deal but still left us $1,200 down on where we should've been if either mathematician could correctly interpret dates.

Angela then kicked into gear as the voice of reason. "Why don't we just go down as if we were booked on today's flight and see what happens?" – the worst-case scenario here being that if they still wanted $2,000, then we were probably just going to have to suck it up… For me, excuses could be made in terms of work, but there was nothing there that was insurmountable. Unfortunately, Angela didn't have that luxury – she had to get back. Anyway, we had a plan…

Hilarity returned to our gathering, mainly gallows humour I suppose, and we reflected on how fate had intervened to allow us one final unexpected hurrah at Billy Bob's the previous evening. Suitably upbeat, after lunch, the guys drove us to the airport. As we scanned the departures area for "our" check-in desk, we spotted a tall, distinguished-looking, moustachioed gentleman in a British Airways uniform. He had a kindly face and smiled as we approached him.

"Hello, how can I help you?"

"Well, we have a problem, and it's entirely our fault, but… our flight was yesterday."

"Don't worry, it happens," he said, guiding us towards a computer terminal.

After a rapid series of taps, he said, "I can get you on today's flight to Gatwick, but I can't get you from Gatwick to Edinburgh. Hold on… Right, you'll have to get from Gatwick to Heathrow for your connecting flight to Edinburgh, but you've got plenty of time to make the connection."

"That's excellent. How much will it cost us?"

"No, don't worry, today's flight isn't full, and I've just transferred your tickets across. You'll only have to pay for the shuttle bus from Gatwick to Heathrow."

Not quite able to believe our luck, we went back to update Fiona and Mirek while he printed the tickets. We said our goodbyes and returned to collect our tickets.

"There you go – enjoy your flight. Now, is there anything else I can help you with?"

Angela piped up, "Will it be OK to take this on the flight?"

For the first time, his smile disappeared slightly as he focused on *that* stained-glass window, swathed in bubble wrap, which we'd kept hidden behind our luggage to this point.

"I'm afraid I can't help you with that – you'll have to talk to the security and check-in staff for that one. Good luck."

We thanked him again and moved to the check-in desk to get our boarding passes and, again, asked them about this pesky window.

"You'll have to ask the cabin staff. If they have room, they can put it in their storage area. Good luck."

Our suitcases were whisked away in one direction as we moved towards the security scanners to put our hand luggage – including *that* stained-glass window! – on the conveyor belt. Before we could go through the body scanner, a security guard yelled, "Wait!" and called us back while pointing to, aye, you've guessed it, that flipping window.

"I'll just make this a little more secure," she said, wrapping another layer of protective bubbles around it with copious amounts of sticky tape. "Right, you're good to go – enjoy your flight." Amazing!

Still unable to believe we'd pulled this off – and full credit to Angela here; it was completely her idea to style it out and see what happened – we sat in the departure lounge reflecting on our good fortune. I think it was only then that we realised that everybody back home was expecting us today.

I can't remember the order of the phone calls, but we had to phone both dads and Ted to explain we'd be a day late and not to worry.

My dad: "Oh, I thought you were back on Monday..."

Angela's dad: "I thought you were back tomorrow..."

Ted: "I didnae ken when you were back!"

So much for people worrying about us! Anyway, we still had one hurdle to overcome – yes, the stained-glass window, though we shouldn't have worried as a smiling flight assistant readily agreed to our request and stored it safely behind her seat. Phew!

Remember, this adventure was in 2006, and I'm writing about it in 2025, almost 20 years ago, so, as an update, you may be interested to learn that the stained-glass window is safely stored in its bubble wrap behind our wardrobe as we still haven't found the "right" place to hang it...

After a couple of months back in normal life, and the tedium of work, Angela and I decided that it would be a great idea to invite our dads out to join us in Italy for part of our summer holiday. This is probably as good a place as any to explain why it was just "our dads"...

The previous year, 2005, we suddenly lost Angela's mum, Ruth. As with my mum's passing six years previously, it was entirely unexpected and came as a great shock, especially, obviously, to Angela. The grieving process is always hard, and I remember how difficult it was for me to mourn my mum while constantly worrying about and trying to protect my dad. For Angela, it was even worse because her dad, Eddie, had been living with Parkinson's for a few years, even though it had only recently been diagnosed, and had become increasingly reliant on Ruth for many day-to-day things, a responsibility that clearly was now going to rest on Angela and her siblings.

Somehow, as we inevitably do in these situations, we carried on as best we could, but how Angela coped over the next few years with an increasingly difficult workload as well as looking after her dad – and her husband! – is a mystery to me. Still, one of the more enjoyable things we could do with both of our widowed fathers was to take them on holiday with us, which we happily – more qualification on the word "happily" later! – did for the next few years.

For that summer then, our plan was that Angela and I would revisit Sorrento for about a week, then we'd hire a villa somewhere in Tuscany or Umbria where we would be joined by the Dynamic Duo – or Gruesome Twosome depending on how we felt at the time! – for a week or so. Then we would pack them off home and recover – sorry, did I just say that out loud? – I mean, continue our holiday elsewhere.

However, the week before we left Dundee, I injured my back quite badly lifting weights at the gym and only had time for a quick telephone conversation with a physiotherapist the day before we were due to fly. She advised me on some stretching exercises that would help, and it was a very slow and old-looking Gordon that shuffled onto the plane. While we were in Sorrento, I could only walk for around 50 yards at a time before I had to stop and do some stretching to try and relieve the pain.

Apart from that, we had our usual great time, which was enhanced by Italy's progress in the World Cup. We watched their quarter-final win over Ukraine in one of Sorrento's many outdoor restaurants before joining the celebrations in the main square, Piazza Tasso, which continued until well after midnight. It was mayhem – thousands of people dancing and singing, and the traditional Mediterranean-style car and moped processions complete with flags, banners, flares and hooting horns. At one stage, we'd considered catching a bus back to the hotel, but when we finally decided we should really go back, as we were leaving early the next day, we actually walked past the bus as it was still caught up in the procession! Indeed, the driver and the one solitary passenger were bouncing around and singing as much as anyone.

The next day I eased my aching body into the hire car, and we set off on the five-hour drive to Macchie in Umbria where we'd rented our villa for the next fortnight. I say "villa" but it was actually just a small townhouse in a very small town. There was to be only the four of us anyway, so we didn't need a huge mansion with a pool, and we actually felt quite fortunate to have located this reasonably priced property. When we arrived, we discovered that, unsurprisingly, all of the photographs we'd seen online had been taken from somewhat flattering angles.

It was OK though, and, amazingly, it was actually owned by a Scottish guy, James. He was friendly enough and helped us settle in. We had a couple of days before we had to return to Rome to collect the two dads, and one of the things we quickly realised we had to prioritise was buying a couple of fans for their bedrooms. It was blisteringly hot, and I was genuinely worried that they wouldn't cope. We had visions of having to book them into an air-conditioned hotel nearby, but, as it turned out, the temperature dropped a little and the fans did their job.

We probably didn't fully appreciate it at the time, but Dad and Eddie were on a great adventure, being 79 and 75 respectively at the time. They seemed quite excited when we picked them up at the airport, although they were clearly tired on the journey north. We stopped for a coffee in a motorway service area and managed to catch the last 10 minutes of Italy's semi-final against Germany, sharing in the truckers' joy at Italy's win. On arriving in Macchie, both dads seemed quite happy with everything, and so the adventure began...

Each morning, my dad would be up and away at the crack of dawn, wandering around Macchie and goodness knows where else, returning just in time for breakfast. Angela had her hands full helping her dad get ready each morning, but once we were all fed and watered, it was time to show them the sights we were already familiar with from previous visits to the area. We were also keen to show them a house we were seriously considering buying...

I'm not entirely sure of the timeline here, but let's have a think... We got married in Sorrento in April 2002 and returned the following year with the crazy notion, "Why don't we buy a house here?" We asked Sandra, our wedding planner, about the possibilities, and she laughed – "Good luck with that – houses here are like London prices." Surely not? Anyway, she hooked us up with an estate agent friend and, right enough, he proceeded to show us a range of houses at ludicrous London prices.

We saw a few things with him but one sticks out – a top-floor apartment in Massa Lubrense, around 5 km from

Sorrento. The setting was fantastic – the entire top floor of an apartment block, with a 360-degree roof terrace overlooking the island of Capri. It needed complete refurbishment and could easily have been developed into two decent-sized flats, but at €650,000 (20-odd years ago, by the way!) it was way, way, way out of our range! It probably would've taken as much again for the refurbishment, so our dreams took a severe dent. Undeterred, we began to think of alternative locations and, when we were planning our visit to Tuscany the following year, Angela started to make contact with some estate agents with a view to investigating possibilities around Siena.

She quickly discovered that Tuscany in general, and Siena in particular, was just like Sorrento – out of our reach. We were advised to look on the fringes of Tuscany, or even into Umbria, so we made arrangements to meet a few estate agents in the summer of 2005. That year, I'd sourced a small hotel in the village of Farneta near Cortona, right on the border between Tuscany and Umbria, and that was to be our base for the following 10 days before we would head down to Rome before our flight home.

A quick aside about the hotel… On our second-last morning, when we went down for breakfast, the receptionist asked us if we were ready to check out. I said, "No, we leave tomorrow." She looked perplexed and while switching between a giant sheet of paper and her computer screen said, "*Ma no, è impossibile, abbiamo 'les petits chanteurs' domani*" – "But no, it's impossible, we have 'the little singers' tomorrow." *Les petits chanteurs* turned out to be a group of Canadian teenagers from Montreal who were on some kind of singing tour of Italy and were due to perform at the local abbey the following evening.

This wouldn't necessarily have been a big deal except that their arrival meant the hotel was fully booked – this appeared to be the opposite problem of my counting the days for our hire car a few years earlier, remember? Somehow, I'd managed to be one day short in my booking – oops!

With nowhere to go and not much chance of being able to find someplace at such short notice, the girl came to our rescue by offering a room that they didn't usually rent out, except occasionally to truck drivers, because it was windowless and in the basement. We gratefully accepted her offer and went off to enjoy our day.

When we returned that evening, there was chaos in the basement as this squad of hyperactive Canadian kids ran riot with, apparently, zero adult supervision. When it was still going on well after midnight, I decided enough was enough and I had to do something, so I dressed and went out into the corridor, where I was greeted with the sight of teenagers flying in and out of rooms at high velocity with much excited squealing and banging and crashing and absolutely no sign of it calming down anytime soon.

One room in particular appeared to be the epicentre, and, as the door was slightly ajar, I could see there were around 20 or more kids in there basically wrecking the place. I kicked the door open and shouted, "SHUT THE F*** UP!" There was an immediate stunned silence as everyone stopped and all eyes turned to me. I then went on a rant about the noise they were making, the time of night and the fact that other guests were trying to sleep.

Two of the older boys emerged from the scrum to square up to me and said something about how I shouldn't be cussing like that, or some such other naïve North American nonsense, but delivered in a quite threatening way. My adrenalin levels were well up though so, without missing a beat, I simply growled, "Don't confuse bravery with stupidity, boys," and the combination of my Scottish accent and my well-practised Dundonian football death stare obviously hit the mark as they all shrank away back to their own rooms without another word.

When we went down for breakfast the next day, *les petits chanteurs* had already left, and the hotel staff were counting the cost of the trail of destruction left behind. Apparently, *all* of their supervising teachers had requested rooms two floors above the kids so that *they* wouldn't be disturbed! Grrr.

Back to the point of our visit to this area, the property search…

The first agent took us on a whirlwind tour of a few places but never contacted us again, and the next one was a bit weird – she was Italian/Australian so we had no language barriers, but she just didn't listen. She kept taking us to places in the middle of nowhere that we'd specifically excluded, solely because she wanted to check them out.

On the days when we weren't being led up the garden path – quite literally! – we were able to be regular tourists and check out what the area had to offer. Cortona being the nearest famous tourist attraction to our hotel made it quite naturally our first port of call. Made famous by the *Under the Tuscan Sun* book and film, it's a beautifully preserved hilltop town with interesting, narrow streets to wander, with beautiful vistas of the Val di Chiana from various vantage points – this fertile valley stretches from the Tuscan provinces of Siena and Arezzo in the north to the Umbrian provinces of Perugia and Terni in the south. From one of those viewing spots, we noticed a body of water in the middle distance and both thought simultaneously, *I didn't know there were any lakes here, I wonder what it is?* After returning to the car and consulting a map, we discovered that it was Lago Trasimeno, Italy's fourth-largest lake. Once we'd had our fill of what Cortona had to offer, we set off to see this watery wonder for ourselves.

Now, ahem, this is where our memories differ – Angela believes that we drove around the lake and that our first stop was in the beautiful lakeside town of Passignano, whereas my recollection is that we naturally ended up in Castiglione del Lago, another hilltop town on the opposite side of the lake from Passignano. Notwithstanding the fact that we both believe we're correct, let's accept Angela's version as it's better for my well-being and, regrettably, I have a scintilla of doubt in my mind whereas "Little Miss Can't Be Wrong" is 100 per cent certain that her version is the right one... as usual.

Either way, it's largely irrelevant as we both instantly fell in love with the area and with the lake, which is strange because neither of us are interested in swimming, boating, kitesurfing or even sunbathing, all of which are the usual pursuits of lake-lovers. Oh well, it's beautiful to look at. Maybe it's because we were both raised, mainly, beside the sea and therefore have some kind of natural affinity with water? Who knows, but it certainly helped to put a degree of optimism into our house search as we prepared to meet the next estate agent.

And in this respect, as is inevitably the case, the best was saved for last. The most helpful agency that Angela had been communicating with didn't actually operate in this area but had suggested we contact one in Castiglione del Lago, and this was to prove a masterstroke. We were paired with a

Dutch estate agent, Pauline, who is now a very close friend, and on our first visit, she took us round a few places and gave us a general feel of the area. We felt we were getting somewhere at last and agreed to maintain contact and try again the following year.

And so, once again we've arrived back at 2006.

We used our first few days in Macchie, before the dads arrived, to hook up with Pauline again and work our way through a list of properties she'd come up with. After we'd exhausted the list without seeing "the one", she said there was one more we could see but that she didn't think it was what we were looking for. If there's such a thing as property love at first sight – which there is because we'd already experienced it in Dundee nearly 10 years previously – this was it!

We both loved the place instantly. Nardelli is a very small *borgo*, a village, which is around 5 miles away from the "county town" of Castiglione del Lago, and a mile away from the nearest shops and bars in the smaller town of Pozzuolo. The house is in the *centro storico*, historic centre, but was only around 10 years old when we first saw it and had been built in a traditional style on an old plot, thereby giving the best of both worlds. The owner had built it for himself and his wife, with no thought of property speculation, and was only moving as they needed a bigger place. We were hooked and went away with some serious thinking to do…

So, back to the holiday and the arrival of our Dynamic Duo…

We visited Siena, Cortona, Florence, and drove around most of Umbria and Tuscany, and the dads thoroughly enjoyed themselves. It was hard work for us at times – particularly when Eddie complained that the roads were too twisty! – but immensely enjoyable too. On the night of the 2006 World Cup final, between Italy and France, we went to a restaurant in Camucia, the modern overspill of Cortona, where we could eat and watch the game on a big screen, accompanied only by the Italian owners and staff. We also had the company of a busload of American teenagers for a while, but they bizarrely left while the game was still in progress – strange people, Americans! All the better for us though, and it was a memorable night, especially as Italy won.

We felt thoroughly Italian and vicariously shared in their joy, figuring it was a little unlikely we'd ever experience that sensation in our own right. They offered us free drinks after the final whistle as the celebrations kicked off, then, as we were about to leave the restaurant, Eddie said, "Well, are we just going home now?" Some chance! We explained what Sorrento had been like after the quarter-final and that, now that Italy had won the tournament, we were unlikely to be able to leave Camucia for a couple of hours even if we wanted to. Which we didn't – bring on the celebrations…

We found ourselves a viewing spot at the corner of Camucia's main crossroads and enjoyed the absolute mayhem all over again – what a spectacle! Being more rural, the parade of honking vehicles included some tractors, a couple of which even had fires burning in their trailers. When we eventually did decide to head home, we drove all the way there like locals, tooting at every passing car and beeping out the "Seven Nation Army" theme that the Italians had adopted and translated into "Campione del Mondo"! Our dads loved the whole experience. Great memories.

As their holiday neared its end, we took them with us when we went back for another viewing of our favoured house. They liked it too, and when they left, they knew we were seriously considering a purchase. After dropping them off at the airport for their return flight, we headed back for the last few days of our villa rental with lots to think about. I had a severe dose of cold feet – which wasn't easy in the temperatures we were experiencing. But, showing absolutely zero sympathy for my agonising – and a complete disregard of my by now legendary and lifelong inability to make a decision when faced with a choice – Angela went spare.

We were in bed when she told me in no uncertain terms that if we didn't buy this house, then we'd just been wasting our time and that we'd have to go through the whole process again the next year. "Do you want to buy a house here or not?" she demanded in a voice that clearly indicated what the correct answer was to be. Harsh!

Maybe she just didn't appreciate that particular character flaw – you know, the one that forces me to die a thousand deaths over the choice of Christmas tree – and just how deeply I felt it. Whatever, the tone of her verbal assault left me in no doubt whatsoever that there was only one decision I could reach that would be acceptable. In the morning, we told Pauline that we wanted to proceed, providing we could reach agreement over the price, and set off excitedly for the next leg of our holiday, which was to be a couple of hours further north in Bologna.

While we were up there, we ventured further into the maze of Italian bureaucracy by applying for our *codice fiscale*, the Italian tax code that's an absolute necessity for, well, just about anything official really. We'd been advised that getting one now would make life simpler in the future should we proceed with the house purchase, but we hadn't reckoned on the full extent of Italian logic. Apparently, although having the *codice fiscale* would make buying a house easier, here we were in a remote government office in Bologna being told that we couldn't have a *codice fiscale* as we didn't own a house. Priceless. We enlisted Pauline's help by phone and, after a conversation that involved a fair amount of yelling and screaming – standard practice in an Italian conversation – we got our *codice fiscale*.

Bologna is a beautiful city, and we thoroughly enjoyed it, but we did have one weird experience while there. Let me set the scene…

One day in the hotel, I was reading my holiday book, *Forza Italia*, by Paddy Agnew, an Irish football writer who'd lived in Italy for many years. It was primarily about football but was also a bit of a social discourse based on his experiences of living and working in Italy. Anyway, in one passage he refers to the common sight of young prostitutes plying their trade in broad daylight on the major arterial routes out of Rome. I related this to Angela, and we both agreed that we'd never witnessed this despite having driven on those specific roads many times – mainly when we were getting lost.

Fast forward to that evening and, on returning from the centre of Bologna to our hotel, I got lost – again! – and was trying to navigate myself back on track through instinct. I actually appear to have quite a talent for this, way beyond stereotypical male bravado and bluff, and will return with more examples later in this book.

Anyway, at one point, as I was craning my neck to read a street sign, I nearly hit a car that was parked in a very strange position. I swerved past, and as I cursed at the lunacy of the parking, my eye was caught by a movement on a central grassy area. "That girl's naked!" I exclaimed.

"Where?" said Angela rather too excitedly, spinning round to see where I'd been looking.

It turned out we'd inadvertently stumbled upon Bologna's red-light area, and, Bologna being a fairly well-to-do city, the Bolognese ladies of the night used their own cars in a complete reversal of what we believed to be the norm – even though we'd never consciously previously considered what the norms of prostitution were.

Angela forced me to go round again so she could check out the spectacle, after which we quickly called a halt to our explorations in case we got arrested for kerb-crawling. Would you believe it? We'd never previously thought about prostitution in Italy – or elsewhere, come to think of it! – and had certainly never seen any evidence of it, then I read about it and immediately see it in action. Then, a few days later when we returned to Rome, sure enough, there they were, all over the arterial routes we'd driven along before yet never previously witnessed. Amazing!

After leaving Bologna, en route to Rome we had one more visit to Castiglione del Lago to complete some paper-work committing us to the house purchase – that was us well and truly buying it then! I'm not going to go into too much detail about the process or other related events as I could fill an entire book just on that. In fact, I probably will, so I guess I'm using this outline as a trailer.

CHAPTER 4

The Italian job

(2007–2010)

Suffice to say that, after concluding the deal, we stayed in our new *casa* in Nardelli for a week in February 2007, doing some decorating and scoping out what else we needed to do before coming back again in March to, more or less, finish off. Then, in April, we returned with our two proud dads to let them see the fruits of our labour and to share and enjoy what they, and our mothers, had made possible for us through their hard work, unconditional love and support, and good parenting. It is absolutely not lost on either of us what we both owe our parents for their endless love, support and encouragement, and for the fantastic upbringings we both had.

So, after that emotional Easter break with our two proud dads, it was back to work – and study! – but Angela and I were also then both looking forward excitedly to our first summer holiday in our new setting. Our first decision was that we would drive from Scotland to Italy – well, it's only around 1,500 miles! Now, back in 2007 we had two cars and pretty much ended up tossing a coin to decide which one we should take. We plumped for our Alfa Romeo, not because it was

Italian but because it was a little bit newer and also appeared to be the more reliable at the time. I say "appeared"...

We planned to head down the A1 then A1/M1 towards London then on to Dover. When we reached the services at Scotch Corner, we stopped for a break, and I noticed some liquid under the car and a bit of metal hanging down. I was convinced that something had broken and that we had a leak, so I phoned the AA. When "the man who can" arrived around two hours later (!), he proclaimed there was no leak and that the bit I could see hanging down was just a loose bracket serving no purpose and doing no harm, at which point he promptly ripped it off.

A tad apprehensively, we set off again, massively behind whatever schedule we had and, shortly before midnight, stumbled into a Travelodge somewhere near Chelmsford. Next morning, we set off for Dover, caught the noon ferry to Calais, then on through France heading – roughly – towards Switzerland. Once more around midnight, and again in the pitch-black, we decided we should really be stopping somewhere soon.

"Where are we?" came the question.

"Where's the map?" came the reply.

"What map?" it dawned on both of us simultaneously!

Yes, we'd only set off to drive halfway across Europe on roads we'd never previously encountered... without a map. (Remember, this was in the good old days before satnav.)

Spotting the lights of a town just off the motorway, we headed into what we would later discover was Saverne, a lovely little place, as we were able to clearly see the following morning. But in the dead of night, with nobody on the streets, trying to find a hotel wasn't easy. The first one we saw had no vacancies, the next one appeared to be open but no one would answer the door, and the next provided our first experience of an unmanned automatic hotel...

Yes, inside the front door was a bare foyer with only a vending machine into which we entered €20 and, in return, it dispensed a room key. The room was basic in the extreme, but it was clean, very cheap, and we were exhausted and would only be there for around seven hours. Next morning, we enjoyed a nice *petit déjeuner* before resuming our expedition, still mapless.

Before we left however, I had to call the garage once more for reassurance as a warning light had now appeared on the dash. "Don't worry," advised the mechanic who'd only serviced the car the previous week, "it's probably nothing, but just take it easy."

"Take it easy"? We were only halfway through a 1500-mile marathon, without a map, and "take it easy" wasn't setting my mind to rest! Anyway, adopting a very laidback French attitude, very *laissez-faire*, I tried to forget about the warning light, the broken bracket and the complete absence of a map...

Navigating our way back on to the motorway was relatively easy in daylight – even mapless! – and so we continued our journey on past Strasbourg towards Mulhouse, before entering Switzerland at Basel, continuing south to the Gotthard Tunnel – at around 10.5 miles, this tunnel is almost the same distance as Dundee to Carnoustie, underground! – before, finally, entering Italy at Como. Then it was on towards Milan and the A1 autostrada – *l'autostrada del sole* – which connects Milan to Naples, before exiting at Bettolle for the final 20-minute stretch on the local roads to arrive at our destination. Yes, after that 13-hour mega stage, we were finally "home". Well, our second home.

On the return journey, we pretty much retraced our steps, though this time we stopped off in Como on the first night. The next day, we made it back to close to Saverne, to another pretty town called Châlons-en-Champagne, and, after checking into a grotty but conveniently available hotel, we set off in search of food just as everywhere was closing. One waiter took pity on us and persuaded his kitchen to do one more meal – *merci beaucoup*! The next morning, we checked out of Hotel Grotty *tout de suite* and went in search of breakfast. In a nice little bar, I went to order coffee and brioche, but after five weeks in Italy, I couldn't remember how to say "*café et brioche*". Worse, I actually couldn't remember how to say it in English either. *Sacré bleu*! Sheepishly, I completed the order by pointing and grunting...

It would be fair to say that Angela didn't appear to enjoy the journey too much. As I'm a terrible passenger, but also because I felt a personal responsibility to ensure our safe passage, I did all of the driving – what a guy! The boredom was too much for her, and she immediately embarked on a campaign of "I'm not doing that again". Then, one day she came up with a masterstroke, from her perspective at least. When we started to plan ahead for the 2008 summer holiday, she said, "Your dad fancied that trip – why don't you drive down with him, then I'll fly out?" Genius, if a little self-serving!

Once digested though, this was a truly fantastic idea, and one I'll always be grateful for. A father-and-son road trip – priceless. Dad was well up for it. I suggested we should take in a couple of things en route, and we eventually came up with a plan to visit my uncle Henry's wartime grave in Ranville near Caen then move on to Paris. Henry was my mum's big brother, killed in World War II while serving with the Gordon

Highlanders – hence my first name! – and nobody from our family had ever managed to visit his grave. After Paris, we planned a couple of overnight stops, then on to Milan to visit the legendary Stadio San Siro, home of AC Milan (and also Internazionale, but we'll not dwell on that!) before rocking up in Nardelli with a couple of days to prepare for the arrival of *la principessa*. What could possibly go wrong…?

Day one of the father-and-son road trip saw a 10-hour stretch ahead of us, as there had been for Angela and I a year previously – Dundee to just outside Canterbury, around 20 minutes from Dover. This time around, with the benefit of the previous year's experience, we'd booked our hotel in advance. The journey itself had its moments, both in and out of the car.

Not long after crossing the border into England, we both – automatically, though predictably and ridiculously – ducked as we spotted a boulder coming flying towards the windscreen. It must've been thrown up by a lorry on the opposite carriageway. Anyway, it missed the screen but smacked into the roof box before – as I was only able to confirm once we reached Italy – ricocheting down onto the roof, causing a big dent and several scratches. Great start!

This was us in a brand-new car, by the way. As soon as we'd decided that I'd be driving down with Dad, I said that I wasn't happy going all that way with him if our car was unreliable, as it had been with us the previous year. So, a couple of months beforehand, we'd traded in our two ageing cars and bought our first-ever brand-spanking-new chariot, a silver BMW 3-series. After the car had been christened by that UFO, the fun continued unabated as, at both our motorway pitstops, Dad managed to spill his coffee quite spectacularly. On the second occasion, only great reactions and a nifty piece of footwork saved me from being covered in it. A sign of things to come? Hold that thought.

By the time we reached Canterbury, a little later than anticipated, our only option for refuelling – us, not the car – was the Little Chef adjoining the Travelodge we'd booked into. Once we'd been fed, after a fashion, and watered, we hunkered down for the night, ready for an early start the next day. As Dad didn't sleep late anyway, I'd booked us on an early ferry from Dover to Calais, and we made it with plenty time to spare. Breakfasting on board, Dad made the unusual choice of a cheese-and-pickle sandwich, but each to their own...

Then we headed up on deck so he could take photographs and some video footage, but not before he continued his coffee spillage theme even more dramatically. As he was wrestling himself out from the bench seating, his camera bag caught his still-three-quarters-full coffee mug and sent it flying over the table, narrowly missing a family sitting quietly at the other end. A quick mopping-up job followed before we retreated – carefully. Thankfully, that was the last spillage incident of the trip, though little was I to know at this stage what was still to come...

Dad was excited by every bit of this trip – and I was excited by his excitement – as he was seeing it all through fresh eyes. As we sped down the motorway, he marvelled at how much better the French roads were than the ones we'd left behind. And he wasn't wrong as French motorways are smooth and quiet and an absolute pleasure to drive on. However, even at this early stage of our adventure, I realised that I hadn't fully appreciated how much work this journey was going to involve for me.

Enjoyable though the whole experience was, it was proving to be very tiring making all the decisions. Every time we went somewhere or had to decide on food or whatever, because it was all new to Dad, he was continually looking to me to decide. I know it doesn't sound like much, but I suppose it's a complete reversal of the parent–child relationship, and I hadn't prepared myself for how all-consuming that was going to be.

Anyway, after a thankfully smooth journey and a couple of uneventful – phew! – comfort breaks, we arrived in Ranville. What a beautiful little town, and the war cemetery was immaculate. The whole experience was quite poignant, and I'm very happy that we did it and were able to pay our respects to the uncle I'd never met.

Our next stop was Buc, a small town close to Versailles, where we would stay for one night before venturing into Paris the next day. Rather than try to drive and, more pertinently, park in central Paris, after we checked out of the hotel, we parked at Versailles railway station and caught the Métro into Paris. We had a fantastic day there, really special, though, once again, it wasn't without its challenges – or drama.

Dad was so fit, keen and enthusiastic that it was easy to forget that he was, at this stage, 81 years old and had some, albeit well-controlled, cardiovascular issues. This vulnerability manifested itself when we went up the Eiffel Tower – it was all very exciting, and he was loving it, taking pictures and panoramic videos, but when we took the lift up the last section, everything took a worrying turn. His blood pressure had, apparently, dropped like a stone, and he was dizzy and unsteady.

We got down again as quickly as possible, and I rushed off to get some water. Within five minutes, he was back to his chirpy self and eager to forget all about it. So much so that we spent the rest of the day horsing all over Paris – from the Eiffel to the Arc de Triomphe, all the way down the Champs-Élysées to the Louvre, then on to Notre-Dame, the Île Saint-Louis and finally up the Left Bank before catching the train back to Versailles. Thankfully, both Dad and the car had survived, so we set off on the next leg of the journey, a two-hour drive to Châlons-en-Champagne.

Next day, we were off bright and early for the penultimate leg, through Switzerland and the Gotthard again, before spending the night in Como. This was a bit more of a relaxing day for Dad after his exertions, and drama, in Paris, and we arrived early enough to take a leisurely stroll around our neighbourhood before settling on a restaurant for our first Italian meal of the trip.

Dad was really impressed, as was I, at my command of the Italian language when ordering. Without Angela as my safety net, I excelled myself, which was just as well as Dad was virtually mute by this time – given that English sometimes appeared to be his second language, two days of French followed by the high velocity Italian delivery had pretty much rendered him speechless.

Now, we'd shared a room in the previous overnight stops, but this time we were actually sharing a bed – very Morecambe and Wise!

Next morning, Dad was up at stupid o'clock as usual, and once he'd finished crashing and banging around doing his ablutions, I sought the sanctity of the bathroom to shower and shave. I'd just started shaving when the lights went off – not an ideal situation, but before I could investigate further, they came on again. I checked I hadn't sliced myself in the darkness and resumed the process only for the lights to go off again. When this happened for the third time, I opened the bathroom door and saw Dad standing staring at the wall, clicking a light switch on and off.

"What're you doing?" I enquired, probably not entirely calmly.

"I'm trying to work out what this switch controls," he replied.

Priceless!

Anyway, after breakfast I thought we'd take a wander around the lake to let him see the sights before we set off for Milan. Little did I know how this would turn out…

After casually strolling around the lake, with Dad in great form with his camera as usual, we went into the town centre just to briefly check it out before heading off. I suddenly became aware that Dad was staggering and looking decidedly odd. He wasn't really able to tell me what was wrong, so, as it was a very humid morning, I quickly hustled him into an air-conditioned McDonald's we were conveniently beside.

After sitting him down, I bought some water, and he seemed to be recovering a little, so I said I'd go and get the car as he was in no fit state to walk any further.

As I walked round to the car park, I wasn't in a good place. I didn't know what was wrong with him or what I should do next. I phoned Angela and asked her advice – she calmed me down, and we agreed we'd just have to play it by ear. When I got back, he was standing waiting for me outside McDonald's and skipped into the car like an eight-year-old. Whatever had gone wrong with him was now magically righted, and he was brand new again. This didn't stop me worrying all the way down the road though…

By the time we arrived in Milan, he'd completely dismissed this second blip and was as keen as ever to see round the San Siro. Thankfully, the rest of the journey to Nardelli was uneventful, and we had a couple of days of settling in before heading down to Rome to collect Angela at Ciampino Airport.

Dad immediately re-established his Italian routine – from the holiday in Macchie two years previously – of getting up extraordinarily early, for us anyway, and hiking into Pozzuolo, where he would have a coffee at our favourite bar, Controvento, before retracing his steps in time to harangue us for sleeping late. Just over a mile in each direction, yet he did this every single day he was there. Remarkable. However, there was one more unwelcome adventure just around the corner…

On the Friday before the Sunday that Dad was due to fly back from Rome, we visited a shop on the other side of the lake. We must've been in the shop for no more than 20 minutes. I was ahead of Angela and Dad as we came back out, and as I approached the car, I could see broken glass – yes, we'd been broken into. Despite my constant harping about "leave nothing in the car", on this occasion, Dad had left his camera bag on the back seat.

So our previously pristine new car now had a smashed window and scratched paintwork to add to the roof damage caused by the flying boulder from day one. Also, Dad's binoculars, camera, video camera and video tapes from previous holidays, which were in the camera bag, had all been stolen. After an hour with the Carabinieri filling out the necessary but ultimately futile incident report, it was a very despondent threesome that trudged back to Nardelli.

Many phone calls to our insurance company followed, and the next day we made our way to a BMW dealership in Perugia to see about getting the repair done. They advised us that they'd replace the window but that we should leave the paintwork until we returned home. In any case, they couldn't do the window until the next week, so we'd have to stick with our temporary solution – an elegantly taped plastic bag – for now. What this meant in practice however was that we couldn't really leave the car anywhere that we couldn't see it. That somewhat limited our movements on the Saturday, then, when we dropped Dad off at Ciampino on the Sunday, Angela stayed with the car while I saw him off. He was upset, we were upset, and we still had the insurance and repair hassles ahead. It's a hard life.

Still, one year on, and in 2009, the plans were being laid again for *Father-and-Son Road Trip II* – the sequel. Selective memory thankfully kicked in and dimmed the coffee spilling, health dramas and general 24/7 care in the community issues, and the boys were all set to give it another go. As he'd lost all his precious Paris video footage in that break-in the previous year, we decided to revisit and attempt to recreate most of the experience, minus the wobbles of course. Thankfully, the day before the break-in, I'd transferred his still photographs to my laptop – to this day I know not why – but the video stuff had disappeared never to be seen again.

The absolute most unfortunate aspect of that was that the stolen camera case also contained some tapes that Dad hadn't yet got round to transferring to computer or DVD, and one of those tapes contained footage of Angela's ancient family homestead in Vallerotonda, near Cassino, that we'd taken Dad and Eddie to at Easter. Criminals don't realise, nor do they care, what pain they cause through their greed.

En route to Paris, I decided to take a slight detour to revisit the Canadian War Memorial at Vimy Ridge – more alert readers may remember this from the previous book, where I had the somewhat discombobulating experience of coming face to face with "G. Craigie" carved into the memorial. I'd given Dad the printed directions again – will I ever learn? – and, as we approached the *péage*, the motorway toll booth, I handed him the correct money and reminded him to say *bonjour* and *merci*. Anyway, he handled that expertly, surprisingly enough, but as we drove away from the booth, we had to make a quick decision on a direction…

"Dad, which way?"

"I said *merci*!" he said proudly.

"Aye, very good, but which way?"

As he fumbled with the paperwork, I had to make a guess due to the traffic behind making their displeasure felt at this dithering foreigner, and… I picked the wrong way – *sacré bleu*! However, as we approached the first wee town where it would be possible to do a U-turn, we spotted a signpost for the "Highland Cemetery". Intrigued by this surprise discovery, we followed the directions and came across this small, beautifully kept war cemetery with mainly Scottish inhabitants. After a quick stroll around, we reversed our route to finally arrive at our intended target, Vimy Ridge.

As I've said before, these cemeteries in France and Belgium are incredibly emotional places, especially when you consider the ages of many of those buried there. It's not really tourism, more a way of paying respect, irrespective of the nationalities. Just a tragic waste which, unfortunately and inexcusably, is still going on in various places around the world as I write this. Politicians are fond of paying lip-service to the "never forget" doctrine, but their actions speak far louder than their weasel words.

Anyway, onwards to Paris, and we horsed round a few of the sights again, using the Métro quite extensively this time to cut down on the walking, and also took in a few new ones for Dad. He just enjoyed wherever we went, taking copious amounts of photos and, thankfully, not too much video footage of his feet, unlike the year before!

We were staying in a hotel in a none-too-salubrious neighbourhood, Bobigny, near la Boulevard Périphérique, the Paris ring-road. It was a decent hotel though, with a secure, gated car park, and only a few minutes away from the nearest Métro station, which would allow us to get into all the main sights in around 15 minutes. The Métro journeys were sometimes challenging in trying to make sure we didn't get separated in a crowd, but everything went well and, once again, it was a memorable visit.

Our arrival was quite funny though as our printed directions appeared to be taking us round in circles without ever getting us closer to the hotel. After a few laps of the area, I stopped the car, grabbed the map, scanned our current position and boldly declared something like, "Right, I think if we turn up there, head in that direction then turn right when we see a petrol station, we'll see the hotel." Dad was unconvinced but, with no better suggestions to offer, agreed it was worth a shot – though his coupon didn't seem to agree.

Anyway, I followed my own instincts and, *et voilà* – how d'ya like that local touch? – a few minutes later we were driving through the hotel car park gates. At which point my bemused dad threw the directions onto the floor and said, "I have no idea how you do that, ye wee bugger – it's uncanny!" – which pretty much represents the highest praise possible from a Scottish father to his son.

After living the high life for a few days in Paris, our next stop was to be Mulhouse, on the French–Swiss border and, when we arrived, Dad was decidedly unimpressed by our accommodation.

"What kind of place have you brought me to?" he moaned as he looked around the prefabricated module that was our Hotel Premiere Classe room.

"What do you want for €19?" I countered, adding, "You're only here for around 10 hours, and you'll be eating for one, sleeping for eight, and showering and changing for one."

This logic was apparently lost on him as he smacked his napper off the metal rail supporting the bunk above the main bed. Not a great start but, as predicted, once we'd eaten in the restaurant then returned to go to bed, all seemed forgotten. The next morning, he had a final whine about the shower, then we left it all behind – literally, as we'll hear later – and headed off towards Switzerland bright and early.

One straightforward, albeit quite lengthy, drive later and we were back in Nardelli early enough to stop off at the local pizzeria before unloading and settling in, both happy to be "home" again.

The next morning, Dad came downstairs looking a bit disconsolate and perplexed.

"Have you seen my chain?" he asked.

"Nope. Where did you have it last?"

"I think I've left it on the back of the bathroom door in Mulhouse!"

I should've known things had been going too smoothly this time around. Yes, he'd taken off his necklace, with Mum's gold locket, and a St Christopher she'd given him, and hung it on the door handle while he'd taken his (apparently) unsatisfactory shower. Then, presumably still disconcerted by said shower, he must've walked out and forgotten about it, and I hadn't noticed it when I'd showered.

"OK," I said, "don't worry, we'll sort this out," while secretly thinking, *This'll be interesting...*

I phoned the hotel and quickly ascertained that the lady who answered had even less English than I had French. She was very pleasant and helpful, however, and somehow I thought that we'd eventually established that they did indeed have the chain so now it was "just" a case of figuring out how to retrieve it. I phoned Angela and asked her to contact Fiona in Texas and ask her if she could phone the hotel – Fiona is a fluent French speaker. She did, and the hotel people were probably mightily pleased to be speaking with someone they could understand and readily agreed to send the chain to Scotland free of charge, which was an extremely kind and generous gesture. So, one email exchange later, the return of the chain by post to my uncle Andy's house in Dundee was arranged. The happy ending was fully realised when Dad next visited Andy and was reunited with his chain and, crucially, Mum's locket and St Christopher. All's well etc...

I think we only had one day of acclimatisation/preparation in Nardelli this time round before setting off to collect Angela from Bologna. Dad and I had enough time to very briefly take in the main sights of that beautiful city before heading out to the airport where we awaited the arrival of *la principessa* – I'd taken to calling her that on these journeys because she was simply breezing through airports with her hand luggage while her serfs were transporting her goods and chattels 1,500 miles to her holiday retreat, then chauffeuring her to said holiday retreat!

However, when Angela appeared through the security doors at Arrivals, there was something distinctly different about her... Neither of us commented; we just greeted her enthusiastically and returned to the car, swapping stories of the last few days. But settling into the journey, I could resist no more...

Looking at Angela in the rear-view mirror, I commented, "It's good when you smile – it's the only way of distinguishing you against the upholstery." Not politically correct nowadays, granted, but a fairly accurate assessment of the consequences of her fake tan gone wrong – the girl was mahogany! Not a great look generally but particularly strange on a naturally extremely pale-skinned redhead.

She laughed and related the tale of how it had all gone wrong on her first, and only, spray tan adventure. Suffice to say that after a few days in the Umbrian heat, our white bedsheet looked like the Shroud of Turin as her "tan" transferred to the cotton sheet, thereby returning her to her natural whiter shade of pale.

As our 2009 Italian summer neared its end, Angela and I plotted a very similar driving route in reverse as, after Dad and I had revisited Paris, we decided it was about time we recreated some of our own Parisian memories. After encountering a three-hour delay at the Gotthard Tunnel in Switzerland, we didn't arrive at our first French hotel until around 2 a.m. – fortunately there was another, this time more modern, automated self-check-in system!

While were registering our arrival at one check-in terminal, we noticed there was a French guy at the other terminal having severe difficulties navigating his way around the technology. Despite being absolutely shattered, we did what we thought was the decent thing and helped show him how to check in. He seemed grateful enough – he certainly growled *merci* as he turned back to his friends with his room card…

It was only at this point that we actually looked at his companions – another guy of a similar age, late 20s maybe, and two sheepish-looking young girls, possibly mid-to-late teens or possibly not. They all disappeared towards their accommodation, and it certainly didn't look like the room was going to be used all night or for sleeping – I think if they could've rented for an hour, that would've been enough… Oops.

Up bright and early – well, early anyway – the next day, we headed off in the direction of Paris and a quick return for me to the hotel in Bobigny. This time around, my familiarity with directions, both to the hotel and into central Paris, allowed Angela and I to concentrate on simply having a good time. We revisited all our previous haunts, and it was an excellent way to finish off the holiday.

Actually, it wasn't quite finished as, en route to Calais for the ferry crossing, we found time to visit both the Canadian War Cemetery at Vimy Ridge and the Highland Cemetery nearby, both of which I'd gone to with Dad on the way down only a month or so earlier. It was great to be able to share those experiences with Angela before we finally headed homeward.

Now that this pattern had been firmly established, plans were soon underway for the 2010 *Father-and-Son Road Trip III* – this was getting like *Rocky*! This time we decided to ring the changes a little and go via Mont Blanc before collecting Angela en route, from Pisa this time, therefore all arriving at Nardelli together.

Mont Blanc is a sensational sight. We approached after spending the night in Annecy, where Dad had no cause to complain about his budget accommodation, particularly as their restaurant served up the most magnificent cheese omelette and chips that either of us had ever tasted. When this huge white vision, Mont Blanc, came into view the next day, it was really quite spectacular, and many photographs were taken before we continued through the Mont Blanc tunnel and wended our way south towards Genoa then on to Pisa. Everything pretty much went like clockwork as we collected Angela and continued on to Nardelli for the latest version of our summer frolics. None of us could know that this was to be the last time…

Dad loved Nardelli and loved spending time with us. Over his times there, he actually became quite a local character, and everyone around us recognised him on his morning treks up to and back from Pozzuolo. Etched firmly, and fondly, in my memory is an image of Dad sitting in the sunshine outside Controvento in T-shirt, shorts and a ridiculous bucket hat that he insisted on wearing, casually reading the iconic pink Italian daily sports newspaper, *La Gazzetta dello Sport*, sipping an espresso – wonderful!

There were two thing puzzling me about this picture, however. Firstly, the newspaper was upside down… when I asked him why, he casually turned it right way up and said, "No wonder I couldn't understand it!" And secondly, I had no idea he liked espresso.

When I told him that, he said, "I don't really – it's a wee bit strong for me."

"So why did you order it?"

"I didn't; she just gave it to me."

"What do you mean, 'she just gave it to me'?"

Now, Dad couldn't speak any Italian, so I had always wondered how he managed to order his coffee, but he'd been doing this every morning, so…

"Well, when I arrive, whoever is serving just puts a coffee in front of me – sometimes it's espresso, sometimes cappuccino and sometimes caffè latte. It just depends on who's serving that day."

"What did you order the first time you came in?"

"I think I just pointed at something."

Mamma mia. Because he was dumbstruck, each barista had just guessed at what he wanted and, because he never corrected them, he got whatever they'd originally guessed at each time they saw him.

Mind you, it's probably just as well he wasn't actually ordering as we'd long ago established that Dad's ordering technique could get him into bother. In fact, we'd first noticed this in a bar in Sorrento with Ted during the wedding adventure back in 2002 – if Dad was ordering one drink then, rather than indicating "one" with his index finger, he would routinely use his middle finger! It didn't get any better if he was ordering two drinks because then he would use his index and middle fingers – so far, so good – but the wrong way around! When we'd discovered this, we'd reckoned he'd have to be ordering eight drinks before he was safe, and how often was that going to happen? Go on, try the hand actions – you know you want to.

Before all of this however, the Easter trip of 2010 had been spectacularly memorable, mainly for all the wrong reasons. Eddie's health had been getting worse, and it was really on this trip that the extent of that deterioration fully registered with us. In truth, it was no holiday for Angela as she was practically on 24/7 caring duties with her dad. Then we were affected by the great Icelandic volcanic ash crisis of 2010…

The morning before we were due to return to Scotland, Angela was busy getting Eddie ready for the day, Dad was still out on patrol, and I was fiddling about doing something or nothing when I got a text from our friend Pauline. "Have you heard about the Icelandic volcano?" she asked, in what I presumed was the opening line of a joke. I turned on Sky News and the full story was unfolding.

Ashen, appropriately enough, I went upstairs and told Angela, "I don't think we're going home tomorrow."

Dad returned full of the joys as usual, until I broke the news to him too. As we watched events unfolding, it became clear that we indeed would not be returning on schedule. In my naivety, I assumed that, being a cloud, it would blow away and we'd be good to go the next day. Not so…

We spent the next week in a state of uncertainty, constantly rebooking our flights only for the blanket cancellations to be extended again. By the time we got round to the Tuesday, five days after we'd been due to fly back, our latest flight estimate had stretched to another 10 days… But when we discovered that the airspace had officially been reopened the following day, another extended negotiation with Ryanair finally secured our return flight for – tomorrow!

The joy of replacing the extended wait of 10 days with just the one was unbounded, and we've never been happier to end a holiday. Which was a shame, as the weather was good, and if it hadn't been for the constant uncertainty day-on-day, we could've relaxed and enjoyed the extension. Angela was also under extremely unfair pressure from her employer to return to work, as was everyone else who was stuck in their holiday destinations – staff and students! – through absolutely no fault of their own. There's something seriously wrong with people who like to exercise whatever power they think they have in situations like that. Honestly, a global crisis is taking place and a few jobsworths are concerned that a wee college in Scotland has a few folk absent? Get a grip!

Anyway, the ever-present worry of what we could do next, and how our dads were coping with the uncertainty, was eating away at us, so it was actually a welcome relief to be finally heading back. I have to admit to being a little nervous on the flight home though. I mean, after a full week of constantly being told how serious and dangerous this situation was, overnight it was all now suddenly OK? Mmm... I kept looking out the window for ash clouds, and at one point, I could see a plane heading pretty much directly towards us and was convinced there was going to be a disaster.

One final anecdote from the ash-cloud fiasco, and a long-overdue (?) mention of the beautiful game...

As the days went on with no positive news coming out about the likelihood of flights restarting anytime soon, me and Dad began to get a wee bit nervous about getting home in time for the Scottish Cup Final in May! Yes, Dundee United had reached the final yet again, and this time round our opponents were to be Ross County.

Some rumours had been circulating about air travel being out of the question for several months yet, so it was indeed a great relief when we were able to get home in late April, even if it was a couple of weeks later than expected. The semi-finals had taken place while we were in Italy, and though we were confident that United would win our game against Raith Rovers, we also fully expected that Celtic would beat Ross County, thus setting up yet another United v Celtic final.

When we heard that the Staggies had caused an upset, our first thought was that it was good news for us, closely followed by the realisation that Raith were probably equally likely to have been boosted by County's win. Indeed, when one of my friends texted to say, "Nothing can go wrong now," that only caused greater anxiety to ensue with the thought that his overconfidence had jinxed us. Anyway, United cruised through 2–0, and we had the final to look forward to as favourites to win... along with the pressure of not daring to lose against the lower-league team. Football, eh?

And so it was that on 15 May 2010, we rocked up at Hampden Park on a gloriously sunny Saturday afternoon to witness the finest sight I've ever seen at a cup final – three-quarters of the stadium was awash with tangerine! Around 30,000 Arabs were there to see United's ninth final, along with the 15,000 or so people down from Dingwall to see their first-ever final.

United were in almost complete control of the game but were finding it difficult to break County down. A 0–0 draw at half-time was probably fair, and we fully expected United to increase the pressure in the second half, though it would also be fair to say that the longer the game went without us scoring, the more nerves were beginning to fray. When David Goodwillie scored with a lob from around 30 yards out 15 minutes into the half, the noise and celebration from everyone in tangerine was just incredible – probably as much through relief as joy! But as every football supporter knows, games can turn in an instant, so we only all really started to relax when Craig Conway scored the second 15 minutes later. When he scored his second and our third 10 minutes after that, then it was definitely party time for everybody of a tangerine persuasion, as we could just savour the last few minutes of the game knowing that, indeed, "nothing can go wrong now".

Apart from the sights and sounds and general euphoria of seeing our team win the cup, it was also a really great experience to finally enjoy a game at Hampden without any bile, sectarianism or general rancour. The good people of Dingwall were there to support their team just as we were there to support ours, and there was no hostility or taunting from either side. I really do wish football was always like that...

The next day, we went along to Tannadice to celebrate as the team cavorted on the pitch with their families, still wearing their cup-final suits, and enjoying the moment with the fans. Many of the players hadn't been to bed and, indeed, many were still... ahem... unlikely to pass a breathalyser test anytime soon. I have photos from that afternoon of my dad taking it all in and really enjoying the moment – something that would take on greater significance within a year – and these are the times that make supporting a football team, and sharing in its ups and downs with your loved ones, truly special and memorable.

One other recollection from this period is about the brutal winters we suffered in both 2009 and 2010. In both years, despite living in pretty much the centre of one of Scotland's principal cities, we were effectively snowed in. Now, living three-quarters of the way up an extinct volcano may well have advantages in relation to some aspects of global warming – we ain't getting flooded anytime soon – but it means that whichever direction we go in from our house involves negotiating a hill. Rear-wheel drive cars are notoriously bad in snowy conditions, so our only option during the periods of heavy snowfall was to leave the car sitting in the street, get the wellies on and walk to wherever we had to go. In both years we had around three feet of snow lying in our street, so even if the car was capable of handling the conditions, it had to be dug out first.

If anything, in 2010, the weather was even worse than it had been the previous year. It sticks in my mind that the snow started around 20 November, and that exact same snow was still with us into March 2011 – the winter was that cold! After around three weeks of being snowed in, all the neighbours independently yet collectively decided one sunny but freezing Sunday that enough was enough and we should at least dig the cars out. There was a kind of camaraderie about our efforts which made it all strangely enjoyable.

However, our frivolous banter was brought to a sudden stop when a huge crashing noise made us all stop immediately. The sunshine had started a bit of a thaw, which had apparently loosened just enough snow on the roof of the house at the end of our street that it started to slide off – the resultant avalanche proved to be too much for the cast-iron Victorian gutters, which collapsed under the weight and crashed onto the stone path immediately outside the front door! If anyone had been standing there, or coming in or out of the door, they would've been seriously injured at best. After checking that nobody had been involved, it was a more circumspect group of neighbours who returned quietly to snow-clearing duties, no doubt looking nervously towards their own roofs. I know I was!

Obviously, this period from 2007 to 2010 wasn't just about sunny holidays and arctic winters – although the evidence presented so far in this chapter would suggest otherwise! – and there was plenty happening in our working lives too.

Angela had left Perth College in 2007 to take up a post at the University of Stirling as a teacher fellow in the Institute of Education, working on their TQFE programme. This involved travelling around Scotland visiting various colleges and educational institutions to support, mentor and assess lecturers who were undertaking their Teaching Qualification in Further Education – hence the TQFE acronym. This was a part-time position with the promise of the other half of the week being educational research work. For Angela, this was a particularly attractive appointment, especially as the role combined two of her professional passions – teaching and learning practice combined with assessment and professional standards.

She really enjoyed the work and the freedom that being home-based afforded her, even if she wasn't that keen on the other home-based skiver she shared an office with – that'd be me! Actually, it all worked out perfectly and, although we didn't know it at the time, was a foretaste of things to come in terms of our working lives. I was still working mainly on the Lanarkshire consortium project until sometime in 2008, combining that with my master's studies, which coincidentally, and handily, was also with the University of Stirling, though completely online.

I think it would've been an ironic twist if the programme wasn't online, since the whole point was to explore, experience and extol the virtues of asynchronous technology-enhanced learning, but I have to admit it took a wee bit of getting used to. One of the course lecturers, Glen, was based in Australia, so on the occasions when he wanted to host something "live" at

7 a.m. his time, we'd be tuning in around 10 p.m. the "previous" evening. He was really good though, and I learned so much from him.

A few weeks into the course, I was actually feeling a bit intimidated by some of the discussions as I didn't understand much of the language being used by both the lecturers and the other participants. I had a conversation with Glen about this, and he easily explained some of the jargon and terminologies being used – most of which I'd never heard before – in layman's terms, which I was then able to translate into my own experiences, and from then on everything was pretty much plain sailing.

Initially, the task of writing essays or assignments of 5,000, 10,000 or 15,000 words seemed really daunting, but after a while, the challenge was more about keeping the word count down! Angela was a massive help too, as she'd recently been through a similar experience with her Master of Education post-graduate degree, the MEd, and was able to keep me right on the technicalities of referencing and presentation as demanded by the university – obviously she was completely up to date with this as it just happened to be part of her day job too. All in all, it was a really worthwhile experience, even if the ultimate irony was that my time working in education would come to an end just at the point where I knew more about it than I ever had before. But we didn't know that then...

Anyway, life being as unpredictable as it is, in late 2007, when it became obvious that the funding for the research part of her post wasn't materialising, Angela reluctantly decided that she needed to get back into a full-time post and so she accepted a lecturer's role at Dundee College. This was clearly a step down for her and, ultimately, the move proved to be a mixed experience.

Like I said before, the Further Education sector is an absolutely vital part of the whole educational offering in Scotland, yet it's often treated as an afterthought by governments. My personal take on this is that governmental priorities are primarily schools and universities – because schoolchildren have parents who are voters, and universities are part of the elite establishment – and therefore colleges are at the bottom of the pile when it comes to allocating resources. Short-term thinking, and the reason why FE is often referred to as the "Cinderella sector".

However, a niche opportunity arose for Angela in 2010 when the quality manager post became available as an internal secondment. Once again, a perfect fit for both her professional interests and skillset. And, by sheer coincidence, I ended up project-managing an initiative within the same college.

This was a similar project to the one I'd previously managed in Lanarkshire, and so much of that previous experience was relevant in this one, which was to design and manage the implementation of an online community portal bringing together the college, community and voluntary education providers into a "one-stop shop" for people looking for learning opportunities. It was actually a lot more interesting – and useful! – than it sounds. But, sadly, like most of these projects, as soon as the initial funding runs out, the organisations involved tend to run out of interest and commitment and, before too long, whatever's been developed is just quietly forgotten about. It's a waste of money, time, expertise and opportunity, but it happens time and time again.

One major bonus for Angela with the quality manager role was that it was based in a college building five minutes' walk from our house. However, since the college at that time still operated from five centres, she would often have to take the car to be able to visit the other buildings. One funny situation that came up one day was when I had to visit the furthest-away centre for a project meeting around lunchtime but Angela had needed the car in the morning – not a problem, obviously, as I could simply walk round to her centre and collect it.

So, suited and booted, I left the house in beautiful sunshine for this five-minute walk. Without a hint of exaggeration, before I'd reached the end of our street, the heavens had opened up and I was immediately drenched by what could only be described as a monsoon – I was absolutely drookit! There was no point in going home to change, as there was no indication the rain was stopping anytime soon, so I squelched onwards to collect the keys from Angela. I'm sure she couldn't believe the sight of her husband dripping in her office – I really did look like someone had hosed me down.

Anyway, I collected the car, returned home to dry off and quickly change then headed off to the meeting. It was still pelting down, so I was still wet when I got to the meeting, just not completely saturated as I had been earlier. Climate change? Scotland's always been capable of demonstrating four seasons in one day!

CHAPTER 5

Orphans...

(2011)

At various points in these scribblings, I've summed up some stories as being "good times" – we should certainly savour those good times while we can, as life can come at you unexpectedly, and it certainly came full tilt at us in 2011…

In the space of 16 days in May, we both became effectively orphaned. We lost Eddie on the 10th and Dad on the 26th. This isn't something I want to relive in too much detail here, but suffice to say, we were both devastated. To lose two loved ones in just over a fortnight was cruel in the extreme and so, so hard to come to terms with. But life goes on, never to be the same again, and our only option is to keep going forward no matter how painful it may be.

Everyone who experiences bereavements knows how much there simply is "to do" in addition to the emotional experience – house clearing and other administrative chores – and we did wonder whether we should go on holiday that year or not. In the end, we decided that there was nothing to be gained by not going, so we resolved to take the break and try to get ourselves back to some kind of normality.

We were very much still in the early stages of grieving, but it was actually something we had to do. Our neighbours and friends in Nardelli had to be told, and of course that was hard, but, with hindsight, it's all part of the healing process. I suppose we entered a sort of twilight zone that summer in the sense that being physically removed from the immediate situation allowed us to, in some way, temporarily forget. Not that it was ever out of our minds, but it maybe just wasn't at the absolute forefront all the time as it would've been had we stayed at home.

And we should never forget the debt of gratitude we owe both sets of parents for getting us into a position where we could buy a second home. It will always be a regret that neither of our mums witnessed it – not that my mum would've gone anyway, being frightened of planes, boats and tunnels! – but it was, and still is, a great source of comfort to us that our dads derived so much pleasure from their visits, and that they were so proud of our achievements.

For me, seeing my dad adopt another country, language and culture at such an advanced age was, simply, priceless. I know I'm in danger of overusing this phrase but... great memories, good times. And, Dad, you weren't just my dad, you were my friend, and that is something special between father and son. Arabest TC, God bless.

Ach well... there's really not too much more to say about 2011. We'll never forget everything that happened, but it's better not to dwell too much on it all...

CHAPTER 6

Back to life, back to reality

(2011–2013)

There may seem like too much detail on these holiday trips, and maybe there is, but some of it is central to how our lives have developed over these years. There are also loads of other stories that may yet crop up… believe me!

And this is as far as my 2012 stream-of-consciousness writing took me – everything from here on in is hot off the press in 2025…

But before we press on, one quick flashback to the summer and autumn of 2011…

Our 2011 holiday – following directly on from the trauma of our bereavements – was also different because it meant that Angela did the car journey with me for only the second time. Leaving all the other stuff aside – difficult, but let's – the summer break was just what we needed. Shortly after arriving in Nardelli, we drove up to Milan for five days, the main purpose being to visit the San Siro again but not on football business. No, this was part of Angela's 2010 Christmas present – we were going to see Take That live!

The opening act was Pet Shop Boys, followed by Take That as a four-piece band (minus Robbie Williams), then Robbie as a solo act, before concluding as a "reunited" five-piece Take That. The whole experience was excellent – a little unexpectedly for me! – but definitely went up a notch when the bold Robbie came bouncing onto the stage declaring, "My name is Robbie f***ing Williams!" and proceeded to give an electrifying performance. He really did steal the show, so much so that when his erstwhile bandmates returned to the stage to recreate the original line-up, it actually very much felt like they were Robbie's backing singers. None of these acts were actually my thing, but Robbie won me over with his performance, and Angela loved the whole thing, which was, after all, the whole point. Excellent stuff.

After another few weeks back in Nardelli, it was time to return to our new normal in Scotland, and back to the reality of house clearances and estate administration that we had more or less managed to put to the back of our minds for the previous six or seven weeks.

Once we were back in Dundee, our "new normal" of life as orphans began, and it would be difficult to overstate the effect the double loss had on us once we were back in familiar surroundings. However, Angela went back to work as the quality manager at Dundee College in mid-August, but my consultancy business was quiet – understatement! – and I had little motivation to do much about it at that stage. I had enough on my plate anyway as I had to clear out Mum and Dad's house in Carnoustie and prepare it for sale.

We'd already been through the process at Ruth and Eddie's house before we'd left for the summer and, difficult though it was, at least there was a team to help out – Angela's brother, sister and their spouses – whereas this time there was just little old me (my brother Tommy having tragically passed away back in 1989), ably assisted by Angela at weekends.

It was arguably more painful for me as this had been my home from the age of 10, whereas Angela's parents' house had never actually been her home since she'd left their previous house to go to university back in 1981. Consequently, I discovered that Dad had never cleared any of my old stuff out – toys, books, magazines, you name it – so the whole process became a rather painful trip down memory lane. On the flipside, rediscovering lots of items that I'd almost forgotten existed certainly refreshed lots of happy memories alongside the sadness and helped me to recall many of the stories that I've revisited in this trilogy – so blame Dad!

Because he'd been a stickler for record-keeping, Dad had kept bank statements, utility bills, and all other kinds of paraphernalia that had no value or benefit whatsoever but still had to be scrutinised and shredded in case there was something important lurking in there – a long and tedious process, particularly on your own.

One day, as I was trawling through this paper mountain, the house phone rang. When I answered, I was surprised to hear our family doctor, Alistair Easton, at the other end. He said he'd been phoning regularly in the hope that he would catch me there so he could pass on his condolences. We chatted a bit about my dad and what had happened, and Alistair said that, when the time came, he would like to go like my dad, still with "things to do". He explained that he always felt that people who still had ambitions, and "things to do", were generally happier and had more fulfilling lives even in their later years, and that he could think of nothing worse than reaching a stage where you had nothing left that you wanted to do. It was a very kind gesture to take the trouble to phone – and to persevere over several months! – and a lovely thought to leave me with.

He'd been my doctor too before I moved to Dundee, so we knew each other well, and he also had a great relationship with my dad. Dad often told me that when he visited Alistair for his regular MOT – always his description! – they would get the medical stuff out of the way quickly so they could chat about what Dad had been up to and where he'd been, often involving Alistair getting a map up on his computer to see where Dad's Italian adventures, and father-and-son road trips, had taken him. For me, that's the essence of a good GP.

Anyway, once the paperwork had been sifted through and disposed of, it was time to move on to furnishings and possessions. Again, Dad had kept so much stuff. I felt so guilty about transporting so much of it to the local recycling centre but… what else could I do? Some bits and pieces inevitably made their way to our house to be "reviewed" later – newsflash: some of them are still there – as we'd done with some stuff from Angela's parents' house a few months earlier – newsflash: see previous newsflash. Other bigger items were donated to charity, and, eventually, the house was empty and ready to be marketed for sale.

I was surprised at how the clearance changed my feelings, yet simultaneously didn't, about the house. Once empty, it was just a building and wasn't "home" anymore. Truth be told, it wasn't home without Dad in it, and it had already been a different kind of home without Mum for many years.

And yet… and yet, I could still see every piece of furniture, every bedcovering and curtain, every book, record, magazine, toy and ornament, exactly where they'd been for years. I could still see Mum and Dad in every room; I could see Angela, and Stushie, and every previous friend or girlfriend. I could still hear my music blaring from my pride-and-joy stereo that had caused me so much anguish to choose. I could feel the excitement and joy of so, so many special times, Christmases and Hogmanays and so, so much more… It was still home.

End of an era then, but because of the time I took to clear the house, the time it took to sell and the inevitable palaver around settling the estate, it wasn't until August 2013 – a full 27 months later! – that everything was finally concluded and we could actually fully move on to our next stage of grieving.

For me, I definitely think that an important part of that grieving process was when I started on this project, writing this memoir/autobiography/travelogue or whatever it has turned out to be – a trilogy so far! – during the winter of 2011. Like I said in the prologue of Volume 1:

Here's the thing, the idea for this book came to me while I was running through an unfamiliar bit of my home town, Dundee. I'm not saying this is a good thing or a bad thing, just a thing. You see, I say unfamiliar, yet I lived there for pretty much a whole year when I was nine years old, and that's a long time when you're nine. Yet still, unfamiliar. And, as my mind wandered while I ran, I thought about the other places I'd lived and how strange it is that you never, or hardly ever, set foot in those buildings again after you move…

What worries me in particular is that just as these memories inevitably become misty in the rear-view mirror, I have only now just realised explicitly that the physical memories are disappearing too. My story is disappearing without trace yet, when I close my eyes, I can see snapshots of the houses I grew up in and the schools I attended, and these images trigger other memories of people and places and events and, well, everything really. I suppose that's what is driving this exercise, that I should revisit everything and get these mental images recorded now before they too are forgotten. Wish my dad had done that…

I don't know about you, but I'm tearing up after rereading those words that were, after all, written in 2011 when so many emotions were still being worked through.

To be fair, if you didn't read the first book, *Rebel Without a Clue!*, then this current book must be a gey slog. But that running thing actually did happen, and a day or two later, after pondering a bit – I do like a good ponder! – I started writing that prologue. After that, pretty much every day, I would do whatever I was doing to try and drum up some consultancy work – emails, phone calls, online research and suchlike – then I would retreat into my past, and my memories, and write a stream-of-consciousness narrative of recollections that finally ended up – after a bit of revision, editing, further research and thought, and newly-triggered recollections – as a 100,000-word first draft of… something!

Now, I'd done all of this without ever mentioning it to Angela, so I wasn't sure what I should do with it next, if anything. It had been a cathartic process just getting the memories out of my head and onto paper – well, screen – and

I really believe it helped me enormously to move on from the double whammy of the 2011 bereavements. I just didn't know what Angela would think, and I didn't know if what I'd written was any good anyway. So, after another good ponder, I decided there was only one way to find out...

I gave what I had a final once-over, inevitably changing and adding bits again – this was my first experience of what the writing process is actually like – and tarting up the presentation to make it at least look like a book, then I sneakily loaded the PDF onto Angela's iPad and waited for my moment...

As we settled into the flight to Italy for our Easter holiday, Angela was about to start reading something while I was sorting out my headphones and getting my musical distractions prepared. I got the PDF up on her iPad and said, "I've got something here I'd like you to read and let me know what you think."

She looked puzzled but agreed, and, as soon as she read the first few lines, she said, "Did you write this?" To which I replied, obviously (and nervously!), "Yes."

I was worried that she wouldn't like it, or would think it was rubbish, or that I'd been wasting my time, or whatever, but I was trying hard not to think too much about that and just trying to lose myself in the music with my eyes shut. Every so often, I could feel a wee bit of movement from her, but I just carried on trying to be distracted.

After just one too many of these "movements", my curiosity got the better of me, and I opened my eyes to see Angela convulsing with laughter. I took my headphones off and said, "Is that good laughing or bad laughing?"

"This is really funny," she said, "so it's definitely good laughing." She read out the particular passage that was currently causing her to disintegrate, continually pausing to laugh more.

Hearing her repeat the words I'd written, and the fact she was clearly enjoying them, gave me an immense feeling of pride – and relief! And I was also thinking, *Yeah, that is funny, very funny actually*. She managed to speed through the whole thing in double-quick time, and when she'd finished reading, she said, "You should definitely get this published." Shucks!

I told her that I'd think about it, and that I'd have to finish it off as there was a lot more to write, and that I didn't know if anyone would be interested... but, in hindsight, that was just the start of me prevaricating over what to do with it – a prevarication that would continue for another eight years! In my defence, I really didn't know if anyone – other than maybe friends and family – would be interested in reading my ramblings, funny though some of them may be. I also really, really didn't know if I wanted to expose myself to the world, especially with some of the more personal stories. I'm still not entirely convinced about that, and yet... here we are!

So, the book project was firmly placed in the "something to think about" category for the foreseeable. And apart from the occasional query from Angela as to when I was going to do something with it, there it would stay until 2020... and you'll have to wait until Chapter 10 for the denouement of this saga. There's another tease!

After that holiday was over, we quickly made arrangements for the summer, and we didn't need to make any plans for an early return journey this year as Angela had decided to take voluntary redundancy from Dundee College and move on to her next chapter... and here's another tease – watch this space!

We decided to change our route for the long trek southwards this time, swapping the 10-hour drive through deepest, darkest Englandshire to Dover to cross to Calais – as I had done since 2007 – for the much more palatable four-hour journey to Newcastle to take the overnight ferry to Amsterdam. This meant that instead of travelling through France and Switzerland to reach Italy, our more obvious route was now through the Netherlands, Germany and Austria, thus opening up new opportunities for en-route adventures.

From the Port of Amsterdam, in Ijmuiden, we had a 10-hour journey down to Munich, where we stayed for a few days. Actually, as with any car journey for us, we stayed a little bit outside the city, mainly for parking reasons, but still only a few stops from central Munich by train. As luck would have it, although it was a reasonably small hotel, its restaurant menu was Italian themed – and very good it was too.

We both really liked Munich – for a major city, the central area is actually quite small and walkable, but still with plenty to see and do. On our first day, a short U-Bahn train ride took us out to Olympiapark, where we walked around the stadium and the site of the 1972 Olympic Games. The stadium still looked pretty cool, and the whole park was really nice to walk around on a beautiful summer's day.

From there, we only had to walk around five minutes to reach the BMW Museum on the edge of the park, which was also very interesting. It's still an ambition of mine to buy a car direct from BMW and collect it from the top floor of the museum and drive it out, a possibility that one of the guys at the dealership in Dundee had told me about. Maybe someday...

After our tour of the BMW Museum, we hopped back on to the U-Bahn to return to the city centre. As we were chuntering along on this train, I noticed the guy opposite, a workie who was half asleep, staring at me. Angela had noticed it too, and I think he must've realised that we'd spotted him staring.

"*Was ist das*?" he asked. Now, even with my less-than-rudimentary German I knew that was "What is that?" but I hadn't a clue as to what *das* he was referring to. Probably through some combination of hand gestures, pigeon German and general confusion, we managed to get him to clarify which particular *das* he wanted to know about. "*Was ist G-A-P*?" was the outcome, whereupon we were able to ascertain that he was curious about my Gap T-shirt! Once again, through some means or other, we were able to explain that it was a clothing brand, and, apparently satisfied but clearly unimpressed, he reverted to drowsing. So much for global brand awareness.

We also wanted to visit one of the famous beer halls, and a wee bit of internet research led us to the Hofbräuhaus, one of the oldest with a history dating back to 1589. It certainly lived up to expectations, with bar staff dressed in traditional Bavarian costumes and carrying the huge glass steins to your table with apparent ease. We ordered one drink but two steins as there was no way either of us was drinking a whole one alone – they hold a litre of lager! Obviously, this inevitably led to another comical photo opportunity for Angela, as her entire face nearly fitted inside the glass when she was drinking from it.

There isn't much in particular that springs to mind about our summer in Umbria that year, but simply being in the sunshine with good food, good wine and growing friendships is certainly nothing to be sniffed at. When our thoughts eventually turned to heading home, we decided again to visit somewhere en route, a mini-holiday if you like, to recover from the stresses and strains of doing no gey much all summer.

Angela's definition of "en route" was certainly a wee bit more flexible than mine as she decided she'd like to visit Vienna. "It's only a wee detour," she said, casually waving her hand to the right on the map we were looking at. That "wee detour" only turned out to be 1,500 miles or so "aff route"! However, it was a great idea that we were both up for, so plans were made. But before we set off, we – the "royal we", Angela! – decided it would be a good idea to buy a garden umbrella to take back home, as you do. It was an absolute bargain and, well, it'll fit in the car, won't it? To be fair, it did – just! – but only by feeding the two-metre-long cardboard box through the ski-hole in the car, where the box then sat on the front armrest, leaving just about enough room for me to still change gear, albeit only with my fingertips! (By the way, that experience served me well on a later journey back from Italy when Angela was yet again unable to resist a bargain purchase, only that time it was a two-metre-long rug...)

Notwithstanding this newly acquired gear-change technique, we duly arrived at a golf-resort hotel on the outskirts of Vienna after an overnight stop in Udine. The hotel was perfect as it had great, secure car parking – particularly important when you don't want your oversized umbrella nicked! – and only a 10-minute train journey into downtown Vienna from just outside the grounds. On our first morning, as we came up blinking into the sunlight from the main train station, I looked around at the grand boulevards – very Parisian – and the ornate buildings, and ridiculously declared, "This all looks very eastern European." In my defence, I very quickly realised my stupidity – Vienna was, after all, the capital of the Austro-Hungarian Empire, about as far east in Europe as you could go!

Anyway, I stand by my assessment of its grandeur, and over three or four days we visited all the sights you would expect to visit – various palaces and gardens, theatres and opera houses, the Spanish Riding School and the Sigmund Freud Museum (probably my favourite) – as well as just wandering around and taking in the general ambience. I'm glad we saw it all, but I wouldn't be in any great rush to revisit – probably too eastern European for me!

Only a few months later, we were heading back to Italy to spend our first-ever Christmas abroad. Now, this was exciting as it would involve driving over the Alps in deepest winter. After the bad winters we'd had in 2009 and 2010 – you'll recall that in both years our rear-wheel-drive car drove precisely nowhere during the two–three weeks of snow – I'd had winter tyres fitted in 2011 only for there to be no snow of any note that winter.

Mind you, that mere detail didn't stop me phoning the guys on the service desk at the dealership:

"I've got a complaint about these winter wheels?"

"Why, what's wrong with them?"

"There hasnae been any snow!"

After they stopped laughing, they assured me that, without me realising anything, we'd been safer all winter because the tyres are much more effective than summer tyres when the temperature drops below 5°C, snow or no snow.

However, not only is it a legal requirement to have winter tyres in Italy between November and April, it's also "highly recommended" in Germany and in Austria too. The German/Austrian version is a strange law really, as although you're not legally obliged to have winter tyres, if you have an accident or even just cause a traffic jam due to not having winter tyres, then not only will you be charged but your insurance won't cover you. Why not just make it a legal requirement to remove doubt? Anyway, having the winter tyres for driving through the Alps gave me reassurance that we'd be good to go.

I watched the weather reports in the weeks leading up to our journey, and parts of Germany and Austria were indeed experiencing significant snowfalls. However, they're much more efficient at snow clearance than us, and by the time we arrived, the roads were perfect, with the snow neatly piled up at the verges. They also clearly use different grit or salt than we do as the roads were also perfectly clean and dry, so the journey south was straightforward. It was interesting watching the temperature drop as we drove through the Brenner Pass though, reaching -15°C I think at the highest point before returning to a much more balmy -6°C as we cruised downhill into Italy.

Our good friend Neno invited us into his family home for Christmas dinner, and it was as interesting as it was enjoyable to experience the different culture and norms. We spent Hogmanay with Pauline and her family, which also added a bit of Dutch culture into our Italian adventure, and it was generally just refreshing to see the sights we'd become so familiar with in a winter light instead of the blazing sunshine we'd become accustomed to.

When we started to think about returning home once again, the weather reports weren't looking particularly favourable – heavy snowstorms were approaching Italy from the north, sweeping down through Germany and Austria. We looked carefully at a range of forecasts and quickly ascertained that the snow was indeed likely to affect every stage of our journey, so some careful planning was required.

Our aim was essentially to arrive at each destination before the snow did, and we painstakingly worked out our route and stopovers with that in mind. Once everything was booked up, we relaxed into the last week of our holiday confident in our cunning plan.

Our first stop was, as had become our custom, Trento, in the north of Italy. Everything was going smoothly until we reached Verona, whereupon it started to snow quite heavily – and unexpectedly as it wasn't forecast until a day or two later. By the time we reached Trento an hour later, it was pretty much a whiteout, and when we got up in the morning... the car was buried in around three feet of snow.

Fortunately for me it was light, powdery stuff, and I was able to clear the car with my hands before we set off on our next stage, through the Alps and quite deep into Germany. Our destination was Limburg an der Lahn, a town just north of Frankfurt, and our journey was scheduled to take around eight hours.

However, the further north we went, the heavier the snow got, and by the time we were in Germany, the conditions were treacherous. To be fair, having praised the Germans earlier for their snow-clearing abilities, this isn't a criticism as they were clearing the roads, but the snow was falling extremely heavily. Thankfully our winter tyres were more than earning their keep, but we witnessed many accidents and tailbacks, and our journey time crept up to more than 14 hours.

Arriving in Limburg safely was the main thing obviously, and we were happy to be snuggled up in a warm bed after a difficult day. The next morning looked similar to the previous one, except that the car was buried under even more snow – and this time it wasn't light and powdery; it was wet and icy! Clearing the car with my hands was not a pleasant experience, but my scraper – and my wellies – were buried deep inside the car. Taking wellies with us was a great idea; leaving them in the car not so much.

Anyway, eventually the car was cleared, and I went back inside to thaw out while the car warmed up too. As we gingerly set off on the next leg, leaving Limburg around 10 a.m. for the four-hour journey to Ijmuiden to catch the ferry at 5 p.m. had seemed like a reasonable plan when we were putting the trip together. However, as we re-entered the motorway network and the traffic crawled northwards on the icy surface, we started to have our doubts. The temperature was too low for the screen washer to work, so, after a bit, I had to stop at a parking spot to manually clean the windscreen. Stepping out of the cosy car onto a frozen pavement nearly ended in disaster as I did my best Bambi-on-ice impersonation – now there's a reference back to Volume 1, though no roller skates were involved this time! – but I regained my balance just in time, cleaned the screen, carefully (!) got back in the car and rejoined the wacky races at a snail's pace.

Thankfully, there was to be no more weather-related drama, and we made the ferry in good time, though we both felt unable to relax until we were actually at the port. However, our crossing was the first of the year, which meant the boat hadn't been heated for a couple of weeks and was absolutely freezing!

The rest of 2013 progressed, initially at least, in much the same way as the previous year. We flew out to Italy around Easter for 14 days then drove back over in May for the summer. There were two particular highlights that summer: the first involved a return trip to Milan, this time to see Robbie Williams purely as a solo act, and again at the San Siro; the second, a few weeks later, was another repeat performance as we drove down to Sorrento for a week to revisit many of our old haunts and experiences, like taking a moped down the Amalfi Coast to Positano and Amalfi itself. We probably would've gone for longer than a week, but we'd foolishly agreed to be back in Nardelli for a birthday party being held in a neighbour's garden – oh well, it's a hard life!

So hard, in fact, that our mini-holiday on the way back home to Scotland that year was a few days on the Côte d'Azur, in Nice. Nice was nice – sorry, couldn't resist that! – and we explored as much of it as we could by foot. We also went down to Monaco for an afternoon, taking in the marina with all its luxury yachts and walking around part of the Grand Prix course which takes place on Monaco's regular roads.

The highlight though had to be the obligatory visit to the famous casino, though the bits the likes of us are allowed into aren't as grand as the bits reserved for the rich and famous. Angela played something or other and won, but nowadays there's no immediate payout in cash – they simply give you a chit to hand in to the cashier when you're finished. She decided that the chit was more valuable as a memento of the day she broke the bank at Monte Carlo than cashing out the €2 prize would be.

The other big undertaking of that summer had been to get all the arrangements in place for later in the year, and yet another adventure…

CHAPTER 7

Transatlantic traipsing!

(2013)

Although she doesn't look a day older than when we first met, 2013 would see a milestone birthday for Angela, and she wanted to mark it with a special trip, to Las Vegas. Now, Vegas didn't mean anything to me, and it wasn't somewhere I'd ever been the slightest bit interested in visiting, but if that's where she wanted to go, then that's where we would go. I thought it would also be a good opportunity to revisit Fiona and Mirek in Dallas because, in simplistic terms, we would have had to fly over Dallas to get to Vegas, so combining the two visits made perfect sense to me, and Angela readily agreed.

Of course, Angela being Angela – in an even more exaggerated repeat of her "slight detour" to Vienna suggestion of the previous year – immediately said something along the lines of, "Well, if we're going all that way, we should really visit your family in Ontario too." Wait, what? We may well be, more or less, "passing" Dallas en route to Las Vegas, but incorporating Toronto too is one hell of a detour!

Anyway, once that had been agreed in principle, I contacted my cousin Scott to inveigle him into some subterfuge around our visit as we wanted it to be a surprise for my two elderly aunts, my dad's younger sisters, Rose and Pat. Scott was on board with this plan immediately and offered to put us up for the week we would spend in Ontario while getting my other cousins organised into keeping schtum in front of Rose and Pat. As we'll see later, very successful he was too.

So, the basic plan was then set – we'd fly from Edinburgh to Toronto, stay around there doing family stuff for a week, then fly on to Dallas and spend a week with Fiona and Mirek, then fly to Vegas for the week incorporating Angela's actual birthday, fly back to Dallas for another week with Fiona and Mirek, before flying back to Edinburgh (via Frankfurt as it was a Lufthansa flight) after our month-long birthday adventure. Here we go then – Toronto/Dallas/Vegas, baby!

We only booked the Edinburgh–Toronto and Dallas–Edinburgh flights during the summer as our transatlantic co-conspirators had advised us that the internal North America flights would probably be cheaper and easier to arrange from there. Scott had also suggested that, based on his previous experience, we should leave booking a hotel in Las Vegas until nearer the time as it would probably be easier to "get a deal". We pre-booked a hire car for the Canadian week, so by mid-summer in Italy, we were good to go for later in the year, leaving Edinburgh mid-October and arriving back mid-November, with multiple adventures and reunions in-between – fantastic!

Our first flight was around 10 a.m., so rather than leave home at stupid o'clock in the morning in order to check in three hours beforehand, we booked a "park and stay" deal at an airport hotel, which really made sense as parking the car for a month would've cost an absolute arm and a leg otherwise. So, after a relatively relaxed – if early – start to the morning, we were finally off on our transatlantic adventure. The flight was good, there were no issues getting through customs at Pearson International or picking up our hire car, and the half-hour drive to Scott's house in Bolton was straightforward too.

Arriving there mid-afternoon, we hung out with Scott for a bit then drove another half hour or so to the seniors' complex – what we would most probably call an old folks' home – where Rose had recently moved to with her husband David. We could've left this visit to the next day, but Scott had secretly organised a family get-together for the following evening, and we thought it would be better if the surprise element was done in private rather than in public.

Angela had bought flowers and, when we arrived at the home, we told the reception staff who we were and that this visit was a surprise, and we asked if one of them would take the flowers to Rose without telling her who they were from. They were happy to do this, and Angela had written a note – "Guess who these are from? See you soon" – in order to keep the surprise going. The staff member came back giggling, saying that Rose was delighted to receive the flowers but was really puzzling over who had sent them.

We waited for another few minutes then went up to her room, knocked on the door and heard Rose shouting, "Just come in, it's open," so we did. Well, neither of us have ever seen someone so surprised, before or since, and after a bit of yelling and screaming in disbelief, alongside tears of joy – I hope – we settled in to catch up and tell her how long this had been in the planning and that her children, particularly Scott, were in on the whole thing. A magic moment.

Mind you, one downside was that unbeknown to us, Rose had actually started the undressing process just before we arrived, so all of this tearful and loud cuddling had been carried out with my 81-year-old auntie wearing only her bra on top – a vision which is indelibly seared into my brain.

At least things were a bit calmer – and fully-dressed – when we attempted to repeat the trick with Auntie Pat. Her and my uncle Jock lived in a sheltered complex but were totally independent within their own flat. There was a secure entry system to the block, so, to keep the surprise going, when Pat answered the doorbell ring, I summoned up my best Canadian accent (!) and simply said, "Delivery for Ferrier," and heard Pat say to Jock, "It's a delivery – you go to the door." So far so good then.

Jock arrived at the front door, and his look of bemusement very quickly transformed into a broad smile as he seamlessly got into maintaining the surprise for his wife. As he walked back into their living room, I heard Pat say, "Wha wis it?" – she'd lived in Canada for 50 years at this stage but still had the same broad Dundee accent she'd left Scotland with. Before Jock could answer, she saw us walking in behind him and, well, similar scenes ensued – not quite as dramatic because Pat was more grounded than Rose and also fully clothed – but emotional and lovely all the same. Great memories, and what a brilliant idea it was from Angela to incorporate this into our trip. Who cares about the detour? The memories are priceless.

On then to the following evening and the great family reunion. Scott owned a pub, the Toby Jug, in downtown Bolton so, naturally, that was the venue for the gathering of the clan. Various cousins arrived from slightly further-flung outposts of Ontario, and it was humbling that so many made the effort to come and see us. Family tales were recounted, and plans made for individual catch-ups over the next few days – it very quickly seemed like we were in for a hectic, but enjoyable, week.

The following days were a whirlwind, but we were really keen to see the David Bowie exhibition which was showing that week at the Art Gallery of Toronto. Scott fancied it too, so we arranged to go together. But on the day, although we kept reminding him that we should really get going to make it in time, he kept delaying and telling us there was no rush because it would only take 30 minutes to drive downtown. Yes, you've guessed it, we didn't make it, mainly because we'd left it too late but also because there was horrendous traffic. Scott, naturally, blamed the traffic.

Taking no chances, we went under our own steam the next day, and it was well worth the visit. The exhibition, which had previously shown at the V&A in London, was described by the local newspaper as including

> *... more than 50 of Bowie's flamboyant and often androgynous stage costumes, including his 1972 Ziggy Stardust bodysuits, music videos, photographs, original album artwork, and handwritten setlists and lyrics...*

and obviously had a Bowie soundtrack playing throughout the exhibition space.

One thing that sticks in my mind is the size of his stage outfits and suits – the man must've been absolutely tiny! His "official" height is always given as 5′10″, but there's no way those outfits fitted a man of that height. I'm sure he must've been considerably shorter than me, and I'm 5′8″...

We spent one evening with my cousin Derek (one of Scott's brothers) and his partner, Carol, at their house in some leafy Toronto suburb, and another with my cousin Ian (Auntie Pat's son) and his partner Simone in a little town north of the city

– though we had to sit through the "excitement" of watching Ian's curling match first. Other evenings were spent either hanging out at Scott's house or in his pub – one "lock-in" turning ever-so-slightly wild with drinking and dancing until well into the wee small hours. The funniest story for me though has to be when we were driving back from Derek and Carol's…

I knew the road back to Scott's, but as soon as we reached the highway, we were confronted with signs indicating that the turnoff we wanted was closed for construction – oops! Whether I missed something in the diversion signs that followed or not is a moot point, but I eventually realised that the road we were on ran parallel to the one we needed.

Now, we had no map and no satnav and, by the time I realised we were up the wrang dreel, my trusty (?) co-pilot and navigator was fast asleep – bless. So, taking advantage of my famous homing-pigeon instincts, I decided to take the first exit heading east if I recognised any of the town names and see where we ended up and, around 40 minutes later – after a cross-country adventure in the pitch-black Ontario outback – eventually hit the correct highway – result! I allowed myself a silent moment of congratulation, as I didn't want to disturb Sleeping Beauty, and eventually turned into Scott's drive at about 3 a.m. – this final movement stirring Angela into partial consciousness as she yawned, stretched and declared sleepily that she just wanted to get to bed.

There were still lights on in the house, and as soon as we opened the car doors, we could hear loud music. Walking up the stairs, we could see that Scott had "a few friends" in, and I've never seen such a transformation in energy levels as Angela instantaneously brightened up and walked into the house already dancing – party!

So, phase one of our North American sojourn ended back at Pearson International Airport as we returned the hire car and went through US customs in this Canadian airport – apparently they do this in a few international airports, including Dublin, to save time at the arrival airports in the US. Now, customs officials, in my experience anyway, are seldom jovial characters, which is probably understandable when you consider the nature of the potential threats they're guarding against. However, the guy we encountered must've missed the training day when they covered "dealing with the public" as he was particularly unsmiling and officious.

This was the first time we'd encountered the facial recognition technology which had only recently, I think, been introduced to augment the previous standard fingerprint recognition. Angela went first and passed through without any issues, then it was my turn, and as I offered my angelic little coupon up for his inspection, he turned away from me to look in Angela's direction, sternly uttering, "Step away from my computer, ma'am."

Angela's scientific curiosity had got the better of her, and she was craning her neck, from what I would say was a respectable distance, to try and see what he was seeing when his technology was doing the business on me.

"Oh, sorry," she said, "I was just interested to see what you're looking at."

"You're not supposed to see, ma'am – that's why the computer is angled towards me."

All of this was delivered unsmilingly and with an underlying threat in his voice – cripes! Despite my better half's intervention, he obviously decided that I also wasn't a threat to national security, and the two of us were allowed entry into the United States of America, which was very kind of him seeing as were actually still in Canada.

The other half of that story is that on arrival at Dallas Fort Worth Airport, passengers are free to continue as if they've just disembarked from an internal flight – there's no further security or custom checks or passport control, just pick up thy luggage and walk. It's a huge airport, so despite being able to go directly to the baggage reclaim area, it probably still took a good 15 minutes or so to find it.

The final surprise for this leg of the trip was Fiona bounding excitedly towards us as we approached the luggage carousel. After exchanging hugs, kisses, screams and laughter, we turned to the carousel only to see her heading the other way?

"We have to collect our luggage," we shouted.

"No, Mirek's already got it in the car, come on!"

Wait, what? Now, if you know this is all happening, then obviously it's very convenient, but I'm sure I'm not the only one to see potential flaws in this arrangement – surely anybody could hang around in that area and just pick out a piece of luggage that takes their fancy and skedaddle with their bounty? Whatever, it all worked out for us, and after more hugs 'n' kisses with Mirko, we were soon cruising up Highway 114 towards Keller and the start of what was bound to be a crazy, fun-packed week.

As usual, this time spent with our friends was full-on and packed with laughter, whether they were introducing us to little towns or restaurants, or whatever, that only residents would really know about, or even if we were just hanging out at their home with their ever-increasing number of cats – Fiona volunteers with a cat fostering centre and tends to hang on to a lot of the little critters.

When they were in Canada, they had three cats, but on this visit I think that number had grown to nine… or possibly more. I took an immediate liking to a fluffy jet-black little kitten called Paddy, and he seemed to like us too as he was forever trying to get into whatever room we happened to be in – if the door was closed, you could see his little paw forcing its way under the door and scrabbling about to attract our attention – 100 per cent cuteness.

Anyway, the downside of this plethora of pussycats was that Angela experienced a very quick, and quite extreme, allergic reaction which no amount of antihistamines seemed to help. The poor girl had to resort to wearing a DIY-style facemask to try and cope, which, for the rest of us, provided no end of amusement as she had to flip it up and down while eating and drinking. Mind you, she managed it, like the wee trouper she is. However, this allergic reaction had probably only served to "soften her up" for what was to come…

One evening, we ventured into nearby Fort Worth, nicknamed Cowtown, to attend a rodeo in the famous Stockyards area. We went for something to eat in the old town first then made our way to the rodeo, held in a vast indoor arena, the Cowtown Coliseum.

I can't say I was overly keen to experience this, but when in Rome, or in this case Cowtown, well it seemed like a good idea at the time. What we witnessed was nothing short of horrific – viewed up close, the rodeo part just highlights how distressed the horses are as they buck and thrash around to try and jettison their rider, and the calf-roping is even worse as those wee things are absolutely terrified as they first of all try to evade the lasso and then suffer their legs getting roughly bound together.

I really didn't want to stay, but that choice was taken away anyway when we realised that Angela's breathing had become increasingly wheezy and we had to leave immediately to get some fresh air. As it turned out, the aircon system in the arena hadn't been working that evening, which meant that the horse dander irritants were unfiltered and ready to attack anyone who'd already been sensitised, including Angela.

Thankfully, after wandering about in the fresh air for a bit, she recovered, though neither of us were in the slightest bit interested in returning to see any more of that cruel example of "sport".

When Fiona and Mirek finally joined us, after being reassured that Angela was OK, Fiona then noticed that her engagement ring was missing. She quickly concluded that it must've dropped off at some point during the evening, so we returned to the bar where we'd eaten earlier – nothing. Then, while Fiona and Mirek retraced their steps to the arena – again nothing – Angela and I went over the route from the bar to where we'd parked the car. Yet again, nothing. All in all, it was a fairly disconsolate foursome during the half-hour drive back to Keller. That mood changed approximately five minutes after we arrived back at the house as Fiona cheerily announced that she'd found her ring… beside the bathroom sink. Although we were naturally pleased that she hadn't actually lost her ring, us three perhaps weren't quite so cheery…

After a week of fun and games, it was time for, what was after all, the main event of this transatlantic traipsing – Angela's birthday trip to Las Vegas. Fiona and Mirek dropped us off at the airport, and a mere hour later, our two-hour flight had delivered us to Sin City – the US is so vast that even this short hop involved crossing a time zone.

A shuttle bus took us the very short ride to our luxurious accommodation at the MGM Grand, a movie-themed hotel at the south end of the Las Vegas Strip, the main Vegas thoroughfare. What a place! When it opened in 1993, it was the largest hotel in the world, a 30-storey behemoth with more than 5,000 rooms and, again at the time of opening, the world's largest casino. The hotel complex covers 465,400 square metres, the 30 storeys reach 89 metres high, and the casino itself covers 16,000 square metres – in anybody's language, this place is ginormous.

Although we hadn't realised at the time, the hotel had just been completely refurbished the previous year, which probably goes some way to explaining just how excellently finished our room was, and massive… obviously. I don't remember which floor we were on, but it was the top of the "normal accommodation" – to go higher required a special key to operate the lift.

On our first morning, I decided to go to pick up breakfast from a Starbucks located within the hotel – it took me 30–40 minutes in total, and that didn't involve leaving the hotel! When I got into the lift, there was a young lady already in – she was on her way down from the "exclusive" rooms higher up. She was clearly participating in the upmarket Vegas equivalent of "the walk of shame", as she was wearing a particularly short and tight-fitting sparkly dress, clutching a purse no bigger than a standard wallet which, presumably, contained a change of underwear at most. I dutifully avoided eye contact and concentrated on the cappuccino and cinnamon-and-raisin bagel to come. I should probably have mentioned that this was actually Angela's birthday breakfast, as our first day coincided with her big day of celebration. Suitably fuelled, we set off blinking into the bright Nevada sunshine…

Walking up the Strip and looking around in wonderment at the sheer scale of everything, our first port of call had already been mapped out as the Paris Las Vegas Hotel, and the opportunity to go up the fake Eiffel Tower. Again, as soon as we entered the building, we marvelled at how big the place was. It wasn't immediately obvious which boulevard exactly we had to follow to find the entrance to said Tour Eiffel, so we decided to ask a guy who was working at a photography stand for directions.

Angela went to speak to him while I was still busy looking around. When I heard his reply, I was sparked back into action as I recognised his accent, so I walked over to join them. Not only was I hearing a Scottish accent, it was definitely a Dundee accent – he was from Broughty Ferry. Unbelievable – the first person we actually spoke to in Las Vegas was from jist doon the road!

After a wee bit of banter with our compatriot, he pointed us in the right direction for the ticket office. He also told us that we would have our photos taken as soon as we reached the top and given a chit to hand to him when we were finished in order to get a memory stick with our photo plus some general views... but he helpfully added that we shouldn't bother as it was a complete rip-off – good man!

As we waited in line – nice Americanism there – for a ticket to go up the tower, I spotted a sign that detailed all the discounts available, including free entry for military, veterans and... if you were celebrating your birthday – bonus! We obviously checked for that particular freebie for the rest of the day, to no avail sadly. There was a good view from the top, particularly of the choreographed Fountains of Bellagio directly across the Strip.

From there, we continued up the main drag, and our next mission was to secure tickets for a couple of the many shows on offer. I know it wasn't my birthday, but my only request for the week was to see the Beatles *Love* show, by the Cirque de Soleil, which we knew was showing at the Mirage Hotel. We may, in fact, have already booked that, so we were now searching for something special to float the birthday babe's boat...

It didn't take us long to come across one of the many ticket outlets spread up and down the Strip, with sandwich boards advertising the "specials" and overly enthusiastic sales agents smilingly offering greetings and advice in a very American kind of way. Normally, I just walk away from this kind of nonsense, but for today at least, this was the game we had to play.

"Our" girl excitedly told us what special deals were available, but none of them were really of much interest. When it seemed like we were probably going to have to choose whichever appeared the lesser of the available evils just for the sake of "the experience", I wandered away, leaving Angela to continue the negotiations. I spotted a sign advertising Rod Stewart's return to his Caesars Palace residency so went back to query that possibility.

"No, sorry, tonight's his first night back after his world tour and it's completely sold out."

Curses! At that, she went across to the booking desk to pick up some details of the shows she and Angela had been discussing. As we examined the available options, including some two-for-one deal that really didn't appeal at all, one of her colleagues called her back to the desk. When she came back, she said, "We've just got a few returns for the Rod Stewart show tonight, so I can offer you those at half price?" – that question mark indicates her tone rising at the end in that annoying American/Australian way that's become far too common nowadays. Excellent news, deal quickly sealed, and a couple of happy wee holidaymakers strolled off in search of a lunch venue entirely satisfied with their morning's work.

Still slightly bemused by our luck in securing tickets for such a big show on Angela's actual birthday date, our only concern was whether Rod was still up to it or not – he was, let us not forget, 68 years old at the time. [2025 update: he's about to embark on his "final" tour at age 80!] I was also slightly worried that he might be showcasing his "crooner" setlist, as he'd spent the previous 10 years releasing a series of *Great American Songbook* albums.

We needn't have worried on either score – the tour he'd just returned from had concentrated on his earlier rock stuff and, as we immediately realised, his voice was as good as ever. What a show! It really was excellent, and a fabulous run through his rock 'n' roll and bluesy repertoire, including his work with the Faces – "Stay With Me" is definitely on my elastic top 10, and that evening's version didn't disappoint – and we really couldn't believe how lucky we were to have arranged that at the last minute and that he was in such great form.

I think the Americans in attendance may have been a little bemused when he started kicking "sakker" balls into the audience – the Japanese tourists near us certainly were! – and they probably didn't realise the significance of the Glasgow Celtic badge on the bass drum… Oh well, nobody's perfect.

During the week, we proceeded to walk our hind legs off in blazing temperatures despite the fact it was November. Another adventure on Angela's to-do list was to fly over the Grand Canyon, not something I was overly excited about because, and let's not beat about the bush here, I'm jist a wee feartie!

I was even mair feart when her negotiations seemed to be rotating towards a helicopter flight – see what I did there? – though that may just have been a cynical ploy to make me accept the small plane option more willingly. [Important clarification – it wasn't.]

At the appointed time, we set off by bus through the desert towards Boulder City Airport, marvelling at exactly how green the golf courses for the rich and famous can be in an area with a severe shortage of water, literally a desert. On arrival, as we watched planes of the type we were about to board take off and land, my feartie tendencies were beginning to kick in again, only alleviated by watching the far more frightening spectacle of the helicopters whizzing to and fro at high speed.

Despite my reservations, once we were in the air, the flight was totally relaxing and a great experience. As is almost inevitably the case, my better half was right again, and this was most definitely a must-do event. We flew over the Grand Canyon, swooping down for a closer look at the Hoover Dam and various other points of interest, and the entire day was just a memorable experience.

In a week full of highlights however, it should come as no surprise as to what I was looking forward to most – the Cirque du Soleil show at the Mirage. We'd already visited the venue to check out the Beatles exhibition in the foyer, so my excitement was already pre-fuelled by the time show-time had arrived. It was spectacular. Obviously I was going to enjoy the music – a mish-mash soundtrack of original Beatles music that had been reworked and re-engineered by their producer, George Martin, and his son Giles for the *Love* album released in 2006 – but the spectacle was just so, well, spectacular! There's no other word for it.

The scale of the production, the acrobatics, athleticism, choreography, lighting, costumes – just everything – was entirely captivating, with so much going on that sometimes it was difficult to know where to look. For a show to be so engrossing that you don't want it to end, even after 90 minutes with no intermission, is a rare experience indeed. Fabulous.

We did our best to cover as much of Vegas as we could, at least sticking our heads into each of the major venues, but it really is a very, very big place. We sampled a few of the casinos, but none of the others matched up to the massive one in our own hotel, the MGM Grand. And it's a 24/7 business – tables and puggy machines were occupied even when we were leaving for our sightseeing trips in the morning.

Our welcome package included two free cocktails at one of the many bars, so, having decided it would be rude not to, we headed down one evening to partake of, and in, the many delights on offer. As the cocktails were of more interest to Angela than me, I left those to her and ordered a bottle of Heineken at $8 – not cheap in 2013!

Two cocktails, two Heinekens and $16 later, we left the bar to try our luck on the puggies – I say "our" luck; Angela was doing the heavy lifting while I adopted a watching brief. Angela identified the machines that worked on 10c pieces – she wasn't interested in the money-making potential of the gambling per se, just extending the experience for a longer time – and started to roll the tumblers. Almost immediately, a waiter arrived and asked what she would like to drink – it turned out that drinks were free while you're playing the machines, even the 10c ones!

OK, that was a welcome bonus, but when the waiter repeated the question to me, a mere spectator, I was extremely surprised, though not so much that I couldn't order another Heineken – rats, if only we'd known that half an hour previously…

The casino was absolutely jam-packed, with a constant throng of new arrivals passing through en route to other parts of the building. What was particularly evident was how many younger women – almost exclusively blonde and skinny and wearing a tight, short, black dress – were heading in the same direction as an equal number of chubby, middle-aged, dowdily-dressed "business" men and spotty, preppy "boys" with GI Joe buzzcuts. This procession made me think of a paraphrase of the old Mrs Merton line, "What first attracted you to the millionaire…"

The seamier side of Las Vegas is only too evident when wandering up and down the Strip, which is probably not overly surprising considering the intentions of many who visit there. Not only blatant soliciting, but begging and scamming are also rife, and very, very obvious. Whether these people are hiding in plain sight or the authorities turn a blind eye is difficult to say, but there was certainly little sign of any active policing going on. It did have its funny side too, of course, like one day while I was perusing a McDonald's lunch menu trying to figure out what might be relatively safe for a vegetarian – whatever it turned out to be cost significantly more than the 99c cheeseburger Angela had settled on – when I realised that a couple of the working girls that we'd passed 10 minutes previously were standing beside me contemplating their order, with a uniformed cop beside them doing exactly the same! Well, a gal's gotta eat, s'pose!

I'll say again, I never had any inkling to visit Las Vegas, but I'm glad we did, and I wouldn't be averse to returning someday, but only for a brief refresher. It really is a microcosm

– though given its scale maybe that should be macrocosm – of everything that's wrong with society nowadays, particularly American society. The gap between the haves and the have-nots is painfully on display as the haves and the have-a-little-bits flagrantly waste money on consumerist crap and cheap thrills in full view of the have-nots. But only by actually being there and experiencing first-hand can it all be truly appreciated. All that being said, we had fun too.

It was then time to return to Texas for the last stage of our month-long North American adventure – and a second birthday celebration as Fiona and Mirek had decked out their house to surprise Angela on arrival. Another great night and a fitting finale to the birthday festivities.

I realise that I've steadfastly refused to divulge the lady's age to this point, other than pointing out that she regarded it as a "milestone", and I'm not going to deviate from that approach now. However, what I will say is that one of Fiona's tasteful gifts was a traffic cone with a speed limit on it… 50!

Making doubly, triply, quadruply sure of plane departure and arrival dates this time around, all too soon it was time to be transported back to Dallas Fort Worth Airport for our flight home. Once again, we said our tearful goodbyes then set off on our final mission of this particular trip… which was to secure an upgrade on our homeward-bound flight. This had all started at Edinburgh Airport a month previously, when Angela calmly asked the check-in assistant if there was any chance of being upgraded as she was celebrating a significant birthday – well, if ye dinnae ask, ye dinnae get! We'd had to build up to this request as it did seem kind of forward, but we'd read many stories of people being upgraded for less so… nothing ventured, nothing gained.

Significantly, the assistant didn't bat an eyelid at the question but just said that we should ask again upstairs with her boarding colleagues. Unfortunately, despite the girl upstairs being equally unsurprised by the question, there were no upgrades available on our flight. The internal flights in North America – Toronto to Dallas, Dallas to Vegas, and Vegas to Dallas – had all been single-class flights, so there was no point in asking the question.

As the last roll of the dice – nice Vegas reference there – we decided on a cunning plan for this Dallas to Frankfurt leg. As we were going to go full-on with this attempt, we decided that a wee bit of eye-fluttering and flirting might help to seal the deal, so it was agreed that if the assistant was female, then I'd ask, and if the assistant was male, then Angela would ask. As luck would have it, the first encounter fell to me…

I chatted with the girl on the check-in desk, had a bit of a laugh with her, then asked if there were any upgrades available as our trip had been to celebrate my beautiful wife's birthday. Once again, she happily responded smilingly to the question but simply confirmed what we'd been told before, which was that she couldn't authorise upgrades but that her boarding colleagues upstairs could if anything was available.

So we really were in the last-chance saloon now – hey, a Texan reference this time – and as we still had an hour or so to wait for boarding, we found ourselves a seat with a good view of the boarding desk, ready to pounce as soon as it became staffed.

After a wee while, a guy appeared and started tapping his keyboard and generally getting organised to announce our flight at the appropriate time. Initially, I was relieved at seeing him as this meant that it was back to Angela to make the approach, which was still feeling a little awkward for us self-effacing Scots. However, after observing his movements and facial expressions, as well as his very precise appearance, we both reached the conclusion that it was more likely he would be interested in me rather than Angela.

Taking another deep breath, I casually strolled towards the desk and managed to read his name badge – cunning little tip for encouraging rapport… you're welcome – before he looked up and smiled at me, asking how he could help.

"Hi, Günther. We're on our way home from celebrating my wife's birthday" – I indicated towards Angela, who, I think, smiled and waved – "and we were wondering if you could possibly upgrade us today?"

Again, unfazed by the question, Günther smiled and replied, "OK, let me check," and started tapping away on his keyboard. "Ah, unfortunately not because we've already upgraded a couple of people to business class and that's now full."

Despite this disappointing news, since Günther appeared happy to continue with our conversation – clearly my flirtatious manner was working – I asked him how exactly upgrades worked. He explained that they could only ever upgrade by one class – so economy to business or business to first – if there was space available, obviously, and that they would always give priority to frequent flyer cardholders, though occasionally it was possible for "special events" like Angela's birthday too. Günther added that it was always worth asking the question as it didn't inconvenience them at all, and they were always happy to upgrade if it was possible and apologised again for not being able to do so this time.

So that was that, and we settled in for the long overnighter to Frankfurt, where we would change for the relatively short hop back to Edinburgh.

Frankfurt Airport is massive, probably unsurprisingly as it's Lufthansa's major hub. Although our hold luggage was checked through, we still had to go through the security system before boarding our Edinburgh flight. As every airport appeared – and still appears – to have their own rules as to what should be taken out of your cabin bag and what can be left in, we carefully studied the advisory notices as we shuffled forward in the queue.

We removed our phones and iPads as directed, as well as the mandatory plastic bag containing toiletries, and loaded them into the trays alongside our shoes and jackets, but as we emerged from the scanner, I could see that my bag was going in a different direction to Angela's. I collected my other bits and pieces and followed my bag to the counter where a very gruff German man demanded that I open my bag. Being absolutely 100 per cent confident that I'd done nothing wrong, I happily unzipped the bag, and he immediately pointed to the one item that was offending him.

"*Was ist das*?"

"It's a speaker," I replied – we'd bought a Bose speaker in Texas.

"Why did you not remove it?"

"Your sign specifies phones, tablets and laptops; it doesn't mention speakers."

He seemed singularly unimpressed by the impeccable logic of my answer and motioned for me to follow him and his colleague into a side room. Angela was watching this pantomime from a distance and had no idea what was going on – I had visions of rubber gloves about to be produced for a strip search!

Fortunately, that wasn't on the agenda as he grabbed what looked to me like a giant cotton bud and waved it back and forward over the speaker before grumpily confirming that I could leave and warning me to follow the instructions next time. Having avoided the "rubber glove and bend over" treatment on this occasion, I elected not to remind him that I *had* followed the instructions but that the instructions were imprecise… I'm no daft, *danke schön*!

CHAPTER 8

Writing our own future

(2013–2015)

On our return home then, as 2013 was drawing to a close, it was once more "back to reality" and time to take stock of what was going on in our working lives. By this stage, I'd been away from full-time salaried employment for around nine years and, although the educational consultancy work had pretty much dried up – to be brutally honest, I'd lost interest in it anyway – I had no desire whatsoever to rejoin the ranks.

Actually, if you consider the relative freedom that I'd enjoyed in the years immediately before becoming self-employed, I'd been more or less autonomous for around 15 years and, in that respect, I'd become almost unemployable. So a change of professional direction was definitely on the cards, but the big question was… what to do? I didn't want fixed working hours, or a boss, and I wanted whatever I did to be location independent too. Around this time, it had become very fashionable to talk about the "knowledge economy", so my thinking was, *Well, I know things, so… how hard can this be?*

I'd always fancied writing, and I'd proved that I could write a substantial number of words in the previous few years

– 15,000 for my dissertation and 100,000+ for what eventually became this trilogy – but that provided only evidence of the ability to produce quantity, not quality. Well, that's not exactly true I suppose as the university had rubber-stamped the quality of the dissertation by awarding me my master's degree, and Angela had said kind things about the book-in-progress, though she may be prone to a touch of positive bias.

So, after a bit of online research, and after picking the brains of a couple of friends in the publishing industry, I decided to start a blog... but about what? After a further period of research and procrastination, I concluded that maybe that wasn't for me...

So, having finally realised that a writer needs an outlet, and that a blog about nothing in particular wasn't likely to be that outlet, I set about reading as much as I could from freelance writers who were making a living from their writing. The first thing I learned was that there appears to be a healthy market for freelance writers writing about, ahem, freelance writing.

One piece of advice that did register with me was to "write what you know" or, at least, write about things that you're interested in. But the biggest thing appeared to be learning how to "pitch" to publications, how to find the correct people to pitch to and how to do all of this in a professional way. Having a background in education meant that I recognised the value of "doing a course", so another bit of research uncovered an online course with the London School of Journalism which appeared to tick all of the boxes and which, a few months later, resulted in the proud acquisition of their Diploma (with distinction) in Freelance and Feature Writing – OK, it's not a master's... but it is with "distinction"!

The course itself was really interesting and a great

introduction to the world of journalism, but me being me I guess, I had a few run-ins with my tutor, Nick. While not denying his professional expertise and his knowledge of the norms of his craft, he did give me duff advice on a couple of occasions. That's not me arrogantly asserting that "I knew better" though; on at least one occasion, I actually did as it turns out – just without the arrogance.

Here's a wee diversion – surely not? – to explain that last bit...

In April 2014, while we were in Italy, I was saddened to read of the death of Frank Kopel, a former Dundee United player who'd been cruelly struck down by dementia at a young age – Frank's condition was diagnosed in 2008, when he was only 59. I was particularly moved by Frank's passing as he was one of the players who reminded me of my teenage years supporting United, and probably because I was in the habit of writing pieces for this diploma course, I decided I would write a tribute and send it off to our local newspaper, the *Dundee Courier*, more in hope than expectation...

It would be a severe understatement to say that I was ecstatic when the features editor replied almost immediately to say, "We'd be happy to use your piece as a second opinion column – thanks for submitting it. Can you also send over a head-and-shoulders pic of yourself, please, and we'll be set?"

A hastily arranged photoshoot was organised – in reality, a comedy show involving Angela and I trying to figure out what a professional-but-not-pretentious headshot would look like – utilising our white *stucco* stair walls as the neutral background. Anyway, much giggling later, a suitable photo was decided upon and quickly sent off to *The Courier* along with my suggested byline.

A short time after – not that I was constantly checking or anything – an email arrived to confirm, "That should do nicely, thanks. We'll be running it on Friday." Friday, as in two days' time? Jeezo, the world of journalism moves at a fair old rate of knots.

And so it came to pass that yours truly's smiling coupon, atop my first byline, was there to greet readers of *The Courier* when they arrived at the centre pages of their favourite paper on Friday, 25 April 2014. Happy and proud though I was, if I had any thoughts that this journalism carry-on was a scoosh, then I would very soon be disavowed of that notion...

So after that exciting distraction, it was back to the final few assignments for the diploma. The next assignment required a couple of magazine features to be submitted. I wrote one about the Italian property market, which my tutor thought was great, and I also sent in the very feature that had just been published by *The Courier*... Let's play the "what happened next" round! It would be fair to say that Nick was a little less impressed with that:

I think I said before that opinion and tribute pieces like this are normally written in-house by senior journalists and are a no-go area for freelancers. In all my 25-year career in journalism, I have not written a single opinion piece and neither have many of my freelance friends. The truth is they are virtually impossible to sell. I know you enjoy expressing your opinion and have a lively and engaging turn of phrase – but this is not what editors look for when they are commissioning work. They want someone who has ideas, has their finger on the pulse and is prepared to write about topical issues. Crucially, they must also have access to sources who can shape and inform a piece. I think you need to step back from this idea that journalism is all about the writer. It isn't. It's about the weird and wonderful world around us and the people who inhabit that world. I can guarantee that the sports editor from The Courier *would have written this piece or he may have passed it on to a former player.*

On receiving these excoriating words of wisdom, I held my fire, briefly, before responding by thanking him for his comments and attaching an image of my article as it had appeared in *The Courier*. I added, tongue firmly in cheek:

Thought you might be interested in the attached PDF... never say never! ;)

To his credit, he very quickly came back with:

Gordon – this is absolutely fantastic! I am more than happy to be proved wrong here. Very well done. You are a great writer, and it is rare for comment pieces like this to be run, which makes it all the more impressive. I hope they paid you!

Once my head had returned to its normal size after digesting this fulsome praise, any residual smugness immediately disappeared when I considered his final words... Payment? I'd been so caught up in the excitement of it all that I'd never even asked the question, and *The Courier* hadn't bothered to offer.

Ach weel, ye live and learn... more on that later! But, seriously, Nick's advice and tutoring had been extremely helpful as there is definitely more to this profession than just being able to write well, and discovering this at an early stage was invaluable. But at least I felt confident that I could do this, now it was a case of building some sort of portfolio and seeing where this was going to take me. Exciting times.

Right then, now that the longer-than-expected diversion is over, let's get back to the Easter/Summer Italian adventure of 2014…

Because we were both now, essentially, footloose and fancy-free in the employment stakes, we'd decided that rather than fly out for Easter, drive out for summer, then fly out again in October, we might as well drive out for Easter and stay for however long we decided. We just wanted to sample actually "living" in Italy for an extended spell, and to experience things that we didn't normally see, like, for example, the International Journalism Festival which is held annually in Perugia – talk about segueing neatly into a storyline! We went to a few of the sessions, over two or three days of the five-day event, and it provided a real insight into many of the issues influencing contemporary journalism. And apart from suffering from a wee bit of "imposter syndrome", I began to feel a sense of belonging within the writing community – onwards and upwards!

Of course, football just had to intervene on this idyllic notion of "living" in a different country without a fixed return date as United were, once again, en route to a Scottish Cup Final appearance…

On the day of the semi-final, when United beat Rangers 3–1 at the "neutral venue" of Ibrox Stadium, Rangers' home ground – who says Scottish football is rigged? – I was outside weeding because I couldn't bear trying to follow the match online. Angela was doing something inside while kindly keeping a check on proceedings and offering score updates out of the window.

When United went 3–1 up with only seven minutes left, I was excited but… I'd seen this film too many times before, and Rangers hadn't been awarded their ritual penalty yet! Anyway, when Angela confirmed the full-time score, I let out a roar that must've been heard in the surrounding towns, never mind just our wee *borgo*! And within half an hour of the full-time whistle, she'd already booked return flights from Bologna to Edinburgh so we'd be back for the final against St Johnstone. What a woman!

I'll come back to the football, naturally, but it was an extremely interesting experience "holidaying" in our own country. We picked up a hire car at Edinburgh Airport, which was strange in itself and all the more so since we'd been given an iconic Italian car, a Fiat 500. We'd only been away for a month or so, yet this feeling of being strangers in our own land still wouldn't go away.

I'd arranged tickets for the game through Keith Haggart, United's commercial director, and was feeling entirely confident that Keith had ensured "good" tickets as he was, and still is, very much a friend. The final was to be held at Celtic Park that year, as Hampden was being prepared for the Commonwealth Games, but when we arrived at the stadium, I was less than happy to find that our tickets were in the very front row – below the level of the pitch! – rather than at a decent distance with a good view. Cheers, Keith! I've reminded him of this on several occasions since – all good-naturedly obviously.

As it turned out, having duff seats was the least of our worries. It was a miserable, grey and wet day, and United simply didn't turn up. We had a good team, with some really talented and exciting young players – Ryan Gauld, Stuart Armstrong, Andy Robertson, Gary Mackay-Steven, Nadir

Çiftçi – but on the day, everyone performed well below their best.

That said, we did have a couple of instances of extremely bad luck – but then every supporter of the losing side will inevitably say that. The truth is simply that St Johnstone didn't have to play particularly well – and they didn't – to win the game, and to win their first-ever trophy. It really was an opportunity missed and a major disappointment, and my mood wasn't helped as we trudged back to the car, absolutely drookit, when Angela said, "Oh well, it's good for St Johnstone though." Too soon, my love, too soon.

Our anti-climactic week was well and truly topped off when we returned to Umbria, as friend after friend approached us expectantly awaiting our triumphant news. Seeing the disbelief on their faces did absolutely nothing to raise our spirits. Ach well, it's only a game… said no football fan ever.

But life goes on, and we were soon back on our travels when Angela arranged another holiday within a holiday. This time it was to be a week in Sicily flying from our local airport in Perugia. We flew into Trapani, picked up our hire car and set off in the direction of Erice, an immaculately preserved hilltop town around half an hour's drive from Trapani.

We'd read – well, Angela had read; I just turn up and do as I'm told – that Erice was one of the most beautiful villages in Italy, never mind just Sicily, and it didn't disappoint. After spending an hour or so in baking heat wandering around its ancient streets, the air-conditioned car was calling for the next leg of our journey, onwards to the capital city, Palermo.

We arrived around 5.30-ish into what appeared to be Palermo rush hour – it later became clear that this was just normal traffic for Palermo. Let's deal with that first – it was absolutely crazy. There appeared to be no rules – lines meant nothing, traffic lights were purely advisory, horns were in constant use and didn't necessarily mean anybody had done anything wrong, and priority rested with whoever didn't blink first. I have to admit that a little bit of me loved it, though I was extremely happy that we were driving a hire car and not our own.

When we finally got within striking distance of our hotel, I could see the entrance to the underground car park but couldn't figure out how exactly we could get into the correct lane to access said entrance. We ended up going round the block three or four times before I finally grew a Sicilian pair and forced our wee car into the correct lane – cue much honking – and managed to reach the sanctity of the car park. On the spot, we agreed that all of our sightseeing in Palermo would be on foot or by public transport, as we weren't moving that car before we had to.

All that said, Palermo itself was beautiful – crazy and disorganised, but beautiful. It was another very walkable city, though we also relented and took the car out so we could visit Monreale, a small town with an impressive and famous cathedral around a half-hour drive from the city, up Monte Caputo. I think we spent three nights in Palermo, so two full days of sightseeing, before heading off again to our next stop, Taormina.

Now this was completely different, another beautiful town but much more peaceful than the big city. Perched on a hill overlooking the Ionian Sea, it's an idyllic setting, though the grumbling presence of Mount Etna is ever present. This isn't a travel guide – though you might be excused for thinking so! – and, just like with Palermo, I won't go into a lot of detail about the sights, but the town centre is really pretty, and the ancient Greek amphitheatre is something special too. We only stayed there for two nights but could have easily spent the entire week. But onwards and upwards – literally – as we had sights to see.

From Taormina we drove up Mount Etna, and just like our visit to Vesuvius all those years ago, it was spectacular. What was weird though was that, despite leaving Taormina in temperatures over 30°C, when we exited the car near the summit, it was decidedly chilly. And unlike Vesuvius's rich red lava dust, Etna's is completely black. I definitely preferred Vesuvius, possibly because it was our first exposure to that type of natural phenomenon but probably also because we were able to walk all the way up to the crater. Etna was spectacular but a bit more touristy, and you *have* to take a cable car on the last leg to the actual summit – at an exorbitant price – an opportunity we declined.

We continued our journey down the east coast of the island to visit Catania and Siracusa, staying overnight at a hippodrome a little bit outside of Siracusa, so for both of those cities, our visits definitely fitted the "whistle-stop" category. Having breakfast while watching racehorses out on their morning gallop was a very pleasant way to start the day, then it was off towards Marsala, taking in the Valley of the Temples at Agrigento on the way.

This was to be one of the highlights of our trip but, sadly, the weather gods – Greek or otherwise – had other ideas. As we got closer and closer to Agrigento, we could see worryingly dark storm clouds growing ever more intense the closer we got. And yes, right on cue, the heavens opened up just as we reached Agrigento. Now, rain we could deal with – we are Scottish, after all – but this was full-on forked lightning and crashing thunder. We decided to sit out the storm in a bar with a great view of the ancient ruins… then finally decided to cut our losses three hours later, with the river under our outside chairs having finally subsided, and reluctantly move on – shame.

Marsala was a nice wee town, and we were able to wander around on a lovely evening in the "calm after the storm" before moving on to our final hotel a bit closer to Trapani ahead of our return flight to Perugia. An action-packed and memorable week, and definitely worth a return visit sometime.

Of course, *the* big event of 2014 was the Scottish Independence Referendum on 18 September. We returned to Dundee at the start of the month because we wanted to be as involved in the campaign as we possibly could – attending meetings, delivering leaflets, speaking to anyone who would listen – in order to help maximise the "Yes" vote. I've believed in the restoration of Scotland's independence since I first became politically aware in the early 1970s, and I even remember my parents being excited when Winnie Ewing won her iconic Hamilton by-election in 1967.

Scotland is one of the oldest nations on the planet, and yet, since being sold out by the "parcel o rogues" in 1706/07, has been reduced to being the last colony of the English/British Empire. This is not the place for a lengthy political diatribe, but I cannot stress enough how passionately I feel about this.

However, in September 2014, we were all excited and convinced we were on course for a historic victory that would change all our lives for the better. Angela and I attended the eve-of-poll rally in Perth, where a jam-packed Concert Hall greeted Alex Salmond and Nicola Sturgeon enthusiastically and left buoyant about the following day.

Thursday, 18 September 2014 was a miserable day, in Dundee at any rate – cold, wet and windy – and we spent most of the day "chapping doors" right through until about an hour before the polls closed. Our task was to ask people if they'd voted and, if they hadn't, to encourage them to do so and offer any support they may need, such as transport to the polling station. We were exhausted and, in contrast to the previous evening, went to bed despondent as the early indications did not appear to be good...

We awoke the following morning to the devastating news that the people of Scotland had voted, narrowly, not to reclaim our country's independence. Unionists will say it was a "decisive" victory; it wasn't. Nor was it a "once in a generation" vote as they have continued to claim ever since without defining what they mean by "generation". The British Establishment had received a real fright, and they were going to make sure Scotland was punished, which they will continue to do until we break the chains.

When David Cameron spoke the following morning, his only commitment was to introduce EVEL – English Votes for English Laws – in a blatant attempt to further undermine Scottish influence at Westminster. There was absolutely nothing to acknowledge that almost half of Scottish voters wanted to be free of Westminster rule. Astonishing.

That entire Friday felt like the aftermath of a bereavement as, like thousands of others, we sat around watching news reports and analysis in disbelief. When Alex Salmond announced his resignation, we both cried, as did many others I'm sure. It was a horrible, horrible day.

Nothing will ever convince me that it was a fair referendum – there were far too many reports of electoral shenanigans for that – and the violence perpetrated by Unionist thugs in Glasgow on that Friday evening just put the tin lid on it. We would surely take a long time to recover from this blow...

And yet, by the Saturday, it became obvious that people were becoming optimistic again, emboldened by the fact that, notwithstanding everything the British Establishment had thrown at our cause, we only required a five per cent swing to turn things around... that meant that only 192,000 Scottish voters had to be convinced to change their mind – that's not a lot in the context of an electorate of around 4,250,000.

As more and more people hooked on to this fact, reports of ever-increasing SNP membership numbers added to this somewhat irrational feeling of positivity a mere two days after such a devastating defeat. The game was still there to be won, and we weren't going anywhere.

To finish off 2014, we were back in Nardelli for Christmas and New Year. We spent Christmas Day with Neno and his family again before experiencing a wild New Year celebration in our Bulgarian neighbours' house – because of time differences, we celebrated Bulgarian New Year, Italian New Year, Scottish New Year, Toronto New Year and Texas New Year... in that order! It would seem that every nationality's New Year festivities include much drinking, dancing and general craziness...

Moving seamlessly into 2015 then, and another – yes, another – wee holiday was on the horizon, as we managed to fit in a wee city break in Warsaw. Once again, a beautiful city with loads of interesting stuff to see and do... and to eat!

Just down the street from our hotel was a traditional Polish "milk bar". These aren't what we've come to recognise from American culture – milkshakes, ice cream, fizzy drinks and frothy coffees – as a *bar mleczny* is a government-subsidised café serving traditional Polish food at low prices. They play an important role in Polish culture and are fundamental in maintaining that connection with the communist era, which only ended in 1989/90.

Angela had read about the significance of the milk bars – like I've mentioned before, she tends to do most of any pre-holiday research; I usually just turn up and wing it – so we were delighted to find this one only 50 metres from the hotel.

Now, although the food on offer in the milk bars is wholesome and nutritious fare, the furnishings are a wee bit more utilitarian and definitely a throwback to times past. They're self-service establishments, and the entire menu is in Polish only. None of this is intended as any sort of criticism as, obviously, clean, functional surroundings with healthy food is exactly what we want in a traditional café, and when in Poland, it's entirely reasonable, obviously, for the menu to be in Polish. That said, any menu in a language I'm not familiar with provides a series of challenges for a picky vegetarian who's also nae affy keen on certain vegetables!

We scanned the huge menu behind the rather stern-looking woman sitting behind the till and relatively quickly decided that we really didn't have a scooby what was going on. But, aha, the wonders of modern technology came to our aid as we decided to take a photo of the menu then return to the sanctity of the hotel foyer and take advantage of the Wi-Fi to translate – genius!

Of course nowadays, more than a decade later, we could simply have pointed the phone at the menu and it would be translated immediately, but, sadly, that particular form of techno-wizardry wasn't available to us in 2014.

A mere 10 minutes later and we were back in the milk bar making a complete hash of the Polish pronunciations and pointing at things, a combination which our straight-faced assistant interpreted stoically before wishing us *dziękuję, smacznego* – thank you, enjoy your meal – and an excellent meal it was too.

On a lighter note, by sheer accident, we also found a small eatery selling the best veggie burger I've ever tasted. After wandering around the old town one day – another one that's beautifully preserved and very walkable – and after passing the Presidential Palace on one of modern Warsaw's wide boulevards, we spotted this poster outside a small café advertising veggie burgers and, as it was around lunchtime anyway, we decided to give it a go. Sensational – a verdict backed up by my carnivorous better half. So much so that we returned the next day to order two burgers each – one to eat right away and one to take on the plane the next day.

Moving on from there, my map-reading skills (?) showed that we weren't too far away from the Polish national football stadium, just across the Vistula River, and a mere 40 minutes or so later, we arrived. Stadion Narodowy had only opened two years previously and was a very impressive, ultra-modern beastie which I was very keen to see inside, and my ever-indulgent wee soulmate agreed we should check if there was a tour.

After checking the exterior for a ticket office or information point to no avail, I decided to simply try a likely-looking door, which appeared to be the main entrance. Result – it opened. We went inside, but there was nobody around and nothing obvious about where to go, so we climbed the stairs to see if we'd have better luck on the first floor. Still nothing, so I started to try doors again, and on the second or third go, one opened. We walked along a corridor, again opening a few doors, then arrived at a set of double doors which were not only open but, amazingly, led directly to the pitch.

This was incredible, and as we emerged from the short tunnel area, we could fully take in the huge arena before us and the pristine green playing surface, freshly cut and smelling as good as it looked. As we stood there for a minute or so admiring our surroundings, we noticed there was what appeared to be a tour group making their way through one of the stands behind the goal to our left.

One of the group, presumably the guide, eventually started shouting and waving their arms. Not fully hearing – and not understanding Polish, a fact that had already been well established – we had no idea what they were saying so continued to admire our view. Suddenly, a guy appeared from the tunnel behind us and asked us what we were doing – he must've been speaking English or I wouldn't remember any of this bit – and I said, "We're just looking at the pitch."

"You can't be here. How did you get in anyway?"

"There was nobody around, so I opened a door then walked around a bit until we got here."

"You shouldn't be here. If you want to take a tour, you have to go the booking office."

As far as I remember, he still didn't tell us where to find this invisible booking office, but that was irrelevant anyway as we'd already seen exactly what we wanted to see and probably at closer quarters than the official tour – and free! He huckled us out of the stadium, and we retraced our steps across the river, giggling away for some time. The accidental finds are always the best.

Meanwhile, back in Scotland, I was still trying to find outlets for my new career in journalism, feature writing in particular. I had a notion for a story I wanted to pitch, but the idea wasn't fully fleshed out as yet – all I had was a random connection in my mind between Dundee United, tangerine football kits, adidas sportswear and the 1974 Dutch national team.

Yes, it's about football, well spotted, but I was still following the advice of "write what you know". I thought that maybe if I could contact someone inside the adidas organisation, I'd be able to arrange an interview and somehow manage to weave all of this into a story that some magazine or newspaper would be interested in publishing, preferably for money this time.

I floated the idea past my friend Mikey, a journalist and long-time editor of the world-famous *Beano* comic – he'd been very supportive and encouraging ever since I started on this venture – and he enthusiastically agreed that there was an idea in there. In an amazing coincidence, one of his friends, a former university flatmate, actually worked for adidas in Amsterdam... and he was also an Arab!

Mikey introduced me, virtually, to Dougall, who readily agreed to try and set up something with the guy responsible for the UK football market. After a couple of attempts, it became clear to him that the guy wasn't interested in helping in any way, so we agreed that we should meet instead at Dougall's Amsterdam office the next time we were passing, which would be as we were heading out to Italy again in the summer of 2015.

We'd already established a good rapport via email exchanges, as we clearly shared a similar sense of humour and had our Dundee United connection and love of all things adidas to boot – great pun that one! But going to the adidas building for what was, effectively, a potentially important business meeting was a little daunting, and I was a wee bit nervous, particularly as that pesky imposter syndrome hadn't yet been fully exorcised.

Having selected a smart casual, creative professional outfit for the occasion, I went through final preparations on the ferry. After disembarking, we had a half-hour drive to the Amsterdam headquarters of adidas, close to the Amsterdam Arena. Dougall was immediately very welcoming and took us over to the open-plan canteen area, where we chatted over coffee and pastries. Then he gave us a tour of the building before we settled down in his office for the "interview". Honestly, by this time it seemed like we'd known each other for years and could talk about anything, but I kicked in to professional mode as I tried to explain what my feature idea was. Dougall said he'd definitely want to read something like that and thought a lot of people would. While that was all very encouraging, I hadn't got any closer to figuring out how to make progress with the idea! [2025 update: I still haven't!]

Now, a good few pages back, I left a little tease about "Angela's next chapter", and this was the year when it all started to come together. Just as writing appeared to offer me a flexible and location-independent alternative to a "regular" job, Angela had been researching something that would afford the same advantages.

Having decided to move into the world of copy-editing and proofreading, she set about formalising her natural talent for this painstaking work by working towards the appropriate professional qualifications. When she started her journey, the professional association was the Society for Editors and Proofreaders and, by the time she'd worked her way up to professional status, that association had metamorphosed into the Chartered Institute of Editing and Proofreading.

Initially, she was dividing her time between working on her editorial business and taking on education projects, specialising in quality systems, but gradually, over the next few years, the education side became less interesting and she was devoting all of her energies to the editorial stuff. And she has quite the portfolio – check out *aveditorial.scot* to see the range of impressive titles that have been polished up under her eagle eye.

See, I told you it wasn't "just" a sequence of holidays. Working from home inevitably means we've had less interactions with colleagues and, thankfully, we'd both become our own boss, so there are simply less stories to tell about situations and people like there were previously.

And that's mainly a good thing, though even in the virtual world, "clients" can still provide challenges. Angela's certainly experienced more of these challenges than I have, particularly as many of the academic books she's worked on have been written by people whose first language isn't English and, on more than a few occasions, she's had to navigate a group of authors who each have a different native language.

The fact that, at the end of the process, a polished, professional academic tome is published and ends up being read in the respected world of academia is testament to how painstakingly professional Angela is in whatever she does – shucks!

It wasn't too long before we were off on our travels again, this time to Budapest in November. We've always tried to go somewhere around our birthdays for a short break – early April for me and early November for Angela – even if it's just somewhere reasonably local for a few days. However, we also usually bemoan the fact that April and November aren't necessarily the warmest of months and, in fact, are usually freezing – we've often floated the idea of having an "official" birthday halfway between our two dates, but that ends up in July when we're always on holiday anyway. So this year the chosen venue was Budapest, and yes, it was freezing!

Budapest is yet another beautiful city with so much to see and do. The Hungarian Parliament Building on the eastern bank of the River Danube is probably the most beautiful government building we've ever seen and is a truly spectacular sight from the opposite shore. It's equally impressive inside, and we took the official tour – no sneaking in through open doors this time – to fully experience its grandeur. As part of the tour, we were able to sit in the public gallery and witness part of a debate, probably not something that's still possible under the current regime.

One evening, while strolling around near the parliament building, we came across a memorial in a little public garden, with candles burning around it, commemorating the 1956 revolution and remembering those killed during the Bloody Thursday massacre. A local approached us and asked, in English, if we understood what it was all about which, obviously, we didn't, so he gave us a very interesting explanation. Once again, an example of man's inhumanity...

OK, three funny stories concerning this trip. Yes, yes, I know – you'll be the judge of that.

On the evening of Angela's birthday, we were strolling around downtown Budapest looking for a nice bar for an *aperitivo* before going for a meal. We chanced upon a wee place with a covered outdoor area with space heating – essential for what was rapidly heading towards being a chilly November night. Drinks procured, toast made, we were sitting making plans for the rest of the holiday, sipping our drinks and generally taking in the backstreet Budapest vibe, when my phone buzzed. It was a text message from a friend in Dundee, but it was immediately apparent that I wasn't the intended recipient:

"Café time again XXX" – accompanied by a photograph. Calm yourself – thankfully not that kind of photo.

I messaged him back: "Are you sure that's for me?" and he quickly replied, "Ha, ha, not unless your name's Kate!" – and the moral of this simple tale, dear reader, is always double-check before pressing "send"!

After that unexpected hilarity, we left in search of a restaurant and came across a buffet-style "eat all you like" place which seemed reasonable. Angela picked up one of their flyers and it turned out to be part of a small Budapest chain, but in one of its partner venues, it wasn't just "eat all you like"; it was "drink all you like" too! Now, neither of us are big drinkers, nor eaters for that matter, but this was too good a bargain to turn down, so we set about finding that one.

It really was too good to be true as, in addition to the buffet food, there was also the option of ordering specific freshly cooked dishes – steak, fish, prawns, chicken… a huge selection – which Angela took full advantage of. She also resolved to work her way through the cocktail menu as far as she could, and I can testify that she managed to give that a good go too.

The choice was a bit more limited for us non-carnivores, but there was more than enough tasty meat-free stuff going on to satisfy me, washed down by a few beers. Having eaten more than we should, and certainly having drunk more than we should, it was two happy, giggly wee Scots that made their way back across the Danube to our hotel. Great stuff.

Being November, the city was beginning to construct its Christmas market just off one of the big squares, Elizabeth Square, which is also home to a gigantic Ferris wheel. Angela's eyes lit up when she saw this. Mine… meh, not so much.

When she declared that we simply had to go on this thing, I tried to gently remind her that I'd actually seen this movie before – Angela always wants to do these daredevil things then immediately regrets it… I can name so many previous examples: CN Tower, various cable cars and funiculars, even the partly open stairways at the Eiffel Tower, among a whole host of others.

That apart, I wasn't keen – it's been well established that I'm just a wee feartie – but I know when it's pointless arguing, so we bought the tickets and waited for our turn to board. The Budapest Eye, as it now seems to be called – back in 2014 it was simply the Ferris Wheel of Budapest – is one of the tallest wheels in Europe at 65 metres high and has 42 glass gondolas which can hold up to eight people apparently.

Happily, we had our gondola all to ourselves as we settled in for the ride. I had the foresight to take a photo of an excitedly smiling yet totally relaxed Angela while we were waiting for the passengers to board the following gondola and, therefore, were still at ground level. After a few others had joined, maybe about five minutes or so later, we'd risen to around halfway up and the mood inside our gondola had started to change. A second photo records Angela's growing apprehension for posterity, and she started to say things like, "Oh, I don't like this," as I'd correctly predicted earlier.

Another few minutes and we were at the top, and the next photo captures the sheer terror in my wee lamb's eyes. Frozen to the spot, she exclaimed, "Gordon, I really don't like this. I'll have to get out. Tell them to stop. It's too high, and it's shoogling around. I don't like this!"

By this point, I'd engaged my wife-whispering mode, calmly reassuring her that everything was alright, it was perfectly safe, look at the view and concentrate on the distance, don't look down, etc., etc., my arm around her, holding her tightly all the while. As we started to turn, she got ever more agitated, but I kept up my wife-whispering while adding that it wouldn't be much longer and it was all good, we'll laugh about this later, and all that kind of stuff.

When we eventually returned to *terra firma*, and her wobbly legs had recovered, she reiterated how scary that had been and how she never wanted to feel like that again. After she'd regained her composure, she asked me, "How did you manage to stay so calm?"

"*Calm*? I was scared shitless, but there was no use in both of us panicking, was there?"

Like I said, I've seen this movie before, and I'm absolutely certain I'll see it again.

CHAPTER 9

To Russia, with love

(2016–2017)

Just to interrupt this whole travelogue theme for a moment, there was other work-related stuff going on too, honest! Just as Angela's business continued to build, I'd finally made a breakthrough with a major magazine title – *The Costco Connection*. Now, this isn't a magazine you'll find in your local newsagent, but according to *The New York Times*

> *As of 2024, the magazine is distributed to 15.4 million households and has 300,000 copies at [Costco] warehouses. It has the third-highest magazine circulation in the United States.*

It also has country-specific issues in the UK and Canada, so it's a pretty big deal. My first few commissions involved interviewing members then writing a short piece to describe their business and their relationship with Costco – I even managed to sneak one in to promote Angela's business.

Bigger commissions came up in the following years – interviewing authors, writing travel pieces – but my absolute favourite was one about vegetarian food, which gave me the opportunity to interview Antonio Carluccio. He was so generous with his time – we spoke for over an hour – and so friendly, no "big-time Charlie" attitude despite his many achievements. Antonio was really interesting, and he was interested in me too; in fact, we spent more time talking about life in general than we did about food, though it was abundantly clear how important good food was to him.

He was 79 when I spoke with him, and so full of life and energy – it was a great shock when he passed away the following year. In stark contrast to Antonio, I also had the misfortune to have to interview a few absolute twats – one celebrity chef and one celebrity "historian" spring to mind, both of whom shall remain nameless here...

Back to holidays again, and in January/February, we started to plan a slightly more exotic trip, this time to Moscow. Through various credit-card deals, we'd managed to accumulate a considerable number of Airmiles and, on checking what could actually be purchased with these Airmiles, Angela discovered that British Airways had divided the world into zones and that the maximum bang for our buck would be achieved by finding the furthest-flung place that interested both of us in the Europe zone.

We very quickly settled on Moscow, and Angela bought flights for May using the Airmiles to upgrade to business class – nice! That was only the easy part done...

Researching part of the world that was still shrouded in a bit of mystery, even in 2016, wasn't completely straightforward, but we tracked down a decent hotel in what appeared to be a good area not too far from the Kremlin, Red Square and other must-see venues. With dates, flights and accommodation in place, the next hurdle to overcome was the visa application, and what a hurdle that proved to be. We found the application forms online and quickly realised the scale of the task – among the many details they required were our parents' birthdates, addresses and occupations, and a complete list of every country we'd visited in the previous 10 years… with dates!

Now, you may think that the Russian authorities could get all of that information from reading this trilogy – cheek! – but there are two problems with that. Firstly, the books hadn't been published at that stage (!) and, secondly, despite what you may be thinking, I haven't included *all* of our foreign adventures – I may have to rectify that…

Anyway, once the application forms had been painstakingly completed and sent to the Russian Consulate, the next obstacle was that we could only proceed with the visa process if, and only if, we had an official invite to visit the country. Wait, what? Yes, we had to secure an invitation from some official source within Moscow, and as the only contact we had there was our hotel, we had to request an invitation from there.

To recap, in order to get the official documentation to enter the country, on flights we'd already booked and paid for on a non-refundable basis, we had to ask the hotel, which we'd also already booked and paid for on a non-refundable basis, to officially "invite" us to visit their establishment… What if they said no? Obviously they didn't say no as, although this procedure seemed unnecessarily bureaucratic to us, this was clearly an everyday occurrence for them. So far, so good…

With all the paperwork in hand, the next stage was to visit the Russian Consulate's visa office in Edinburgh to hand the documents over, be eyeballed and quizzed by the staff, and pay them whatever they demanded for the pleasure. After telling the security guard why we were there, we were allowed to enter the dimly lit and silent interior and told to wait until we were called.

I think there were two, possibly three, women sitting behind large, dark, wooden desks on the opposite side of the room, and after a few minutes, one of them motioned for us to approach. She looked at us unsmilingly and asked for our paperwork and passports, which she then studied meticulously before turning to a photocopier behind her desk and duplicating everything we'd handed over. In an ill-judged attempt to break the silence and lighten the mood, one of us commented that this wasn't the easiest of application processes, which was met with a steely stare.

Eventually, she sternly replied, "It is the same for people from my country coming here," and handed us a receipt. "Bring that back here in two weeks to collect your visa, if it is approved. You will be given an appointment by email."

"And our passports?"

"You'll get them back with the visa!"

Two weeks? *If* it's approved? And you're keeping our passports?

We thanked our stony-faced blonde friend and said our goodbyes – as in, *we* both said goodbye; she just stared at us – and returned to the car park in sunny Leith completely bemused by what had just taken place. Anything could now be happening with our passports, and we still didn't have confirmation that our Moscow adventure was a go-go.

Thankfully, we did receive the thumbs-up email within about a week, along with an appointment to return and collect the visas the following week. We were taking nothing for granted until that crucial stamp was in our passports, so, as Angela was working, I went through by myself to collect whatever I had to collect.

I don't know if blondie remembered me or not, but she was no less unfriendly on this occasion as she pulled an envelope out from a pile on her desk, scrutinised the paperwork – again – checked that the visa stamps were inside and pushed the passports towards me.

"Is that everything done then?"

"Yes. Goodbye."

Jeezo! Anyway, that was that, and we were finally clear to look forward to visiting a city that had long fascinated both of us in only a couple of months' time.

We flew out on 9 May, a significant date in the Russian calendar but of which we were blissfully unaware before arrival. First up was a shuttle flight to Heathrow, where we had a couple of hours to kill before our departure for Moscow. Having upgraded to business class, we had the use of the executive lounge, so we got to experience "how the other half live". Having already had breakfast, then coffee and a croissant on the shuttle, we couldn't fully indulge in the delights on offer in the lounge but managed to sample enough to, literally, get a taste. We were also mindful that we would soon enough be having lunch on the plane...

When we boarded, we were quickly like the proverbial kids in a sweetshop, investigating all the luxuries and hidden facilities that we never get to see when flying in "cattle class" – loads of space, swivelling armchairs that convert to flat beds at the touch of a switch, a "goodie bag" with everything you could possibly need for a longish flight, and a plush, freshly laundered blanket.

As we settled in – this is all before take-off mind – a steward arrived and offered us a welcome glass of Kir Royale.

Don't mind if we do! After a swiftly delivered refresh of the glass, everything was cleared away for take-off and we were finally on our way, with approximately four hours of business-class pampering ahead of us.

Immediately the seat belt signs were off, having reached cruising altitude, the guy across the aisle from us flattened his seat, pulled his blanket over his head and settled down to sleep. When the steward appeared again shortly afterwards with the lunch menus, he made it perfectly clear to him that he didn't want to be disturbed for the rest of the flight – no lunch, no drinks, just leave me alone – clearly not a first-time pampered puss. Others further down the cabin had done the same, but that just meant the stewards would have more time to tend to the whims of us clearly and obviously business-class newbies.

After enjoying a sumptuous three-course lunch, with a choice of wines, we explored the films available for viewing on our widescreen monitors and settled in for a relaxing afternoon. Fully fed and watered – possibly overwatered – I said to Angela, "I think when we get offered more wine, we should probably refuse, or we'll be completely stocious when we reach Moscow," an observation she was in complete agreement with.

A short time later, the steward reappeared and offered me a top-up. "No thank you." Then he turned to Angela. "Yes please!" Whatever happened to solidarity? Thank goodness then that at least one of was, more or less, fully *compos mentis* when we arrived at Domodedovo Airport as there were challenges ahead…

Normally, going through security on arrival at a foreign airport is a sobering experience, and rightly so as the staff have an important job to do in scrutinising the people entering their country. This, however, was more intimidating than usual because every single member of staff was in military uniform and all of the signage was indecipherable to us as everything was in the Cyrillic alphabet – that's not a complaint, just a recognition that we could make neither head nor tail of most of it, as we'll elaborate on later.

Anyway, we finally made it through and, reunited with our luggage, traipsed through the terminal building looking hopefully for the taxi driver we'd booked proffering a sign using some combination of our names...

Now, I said "hopefully" as I did have my doubts about this part of the plan. Having already ascertained that taking a train involved at least one change, and knowing that language and general unfamiliarity would make life difficult, I'd been in discussion via email with the hotel about arranging a taxi. This had been agreed in principle but, crucially, we hadn't received confirmation before we left home.

As we wandered around hoping for some divine inspiration, we kept getting approached by a man, who spoke perfect English, asking if we needed a taxi. We told him a few times that one was arranged but, probably on his fourth or fifth approach, he eventually said, "Your taxi is not coming – let me help." By then, we'd accepted this increasingly obvious fact too, so we asked him how much it would cost and he gave some ridiculous figure, which we refused and walked away.

On his next approach, he smiled and offered us a reduced price which, again, we refused. I told him what we'd agreed with the hotel, and he just said, "But that taxi isn't here..." We walked away again. But this time he followed us and said, "OK, OK, I'll do it for that price," and this time we readily accepted.

We then saw him in action – he walked across to one of the taxi drivers, gave him some money, then came back to us, put our cases in the car boot and asked for the price we'd agreed. Who said entrepreneurialism didn't exist in Russia! With that, and handshakes all round, our smiling taxi driver whisked us off towards central Moscow, a journey which took a little more than an hour, with the traffic getting heavier as we got closer to our hotel. We didn't think too much about this as it was a big city and around 6 p.m., so we just presumed this was normal.

After settling into the hotel and discovering that we'd received an email while we were flying asking if we still wanted them to arrange a taxi – the person dealing with it had been off over the weekend and only saw our request that morning – we were told that 9 May is a huge event in Moscow – Victory Day. Every year, there's a huge parade in Red Square commemorating the Red Army's defeat of the Nazis in World War II, which the Russians call the Great Patriotic War.

We'd missed the military parade and fly-past, but the entire day and evening is a big deal. It's a national holiday, and it seemed to us like the whole of Moscow was on the streets in and around Red Square when we arrived. Me being me, I loved the fact that almost every single person was wearing a tangerine-and-black ribbon! Unfortunately for us as Scots, it's called the Saint George ribbon, but it's a symbol of that victory and represents both patriotism and the memory of those who were sacrificed.

As darkness fell, it was particularly emotional around the eternal flame, and I noticed people going forward towards the flame – I decided to have a closer look myself only to find my path blocked by a very grumpy army officer. When I somehow managed to indicate that I only wanted to do what the others were doing, she started to finger the trigger on her sub-machine gun, so I decided maybe it would be best to apologise and retreat!

It turned out that you could only approach the flame if you were carrying a rose to place respectfully in the growing pile around the flame. Having bought a rose from a handily positioned vendor (!), we returned and passed my would-be assassin without further incident, though I still kept a wary eye on her.

Next morning, we were up bright and early and off to find a guided walking tour Angela had read about. Our guide was a young Muscovite, probably around 24, and she took the gathered group off on a tour of many of the centrally located sites of interest, explaining the history and significance in perfect English, albeit with an American accent.

She was excellent and spoke of how things had changed even since her childhood. One story she told was of when her dad had been on a business trip to "the West" and had smuggled back a Mars Bar for his kids to share – *a* Mars Bar! – as a treat. I think she had three siblings, so her dad carefully cut the Mars Bar into four pieces, which each child gratefully received. Her siblings had immediately devoured the sweet morsel, but she'd wanted to make her piece last, so she'd hid it in the fridge and only nibbled off a small piece every evening. If she was only around 24 in 2016, this must've been a typical Russian experience even into the mid-1990s – incredible.

When the tour finished in Red Square, she told us a joke about a Russian and an American standing exactly where we were, outside the Kremlin, debating democracy. The American said, "I live in a democracy and I'm free to say whatever I want. I can stand outside our parliament building and shout, 'The American President is an idiot,' and nothing would happen to me." The Russian replied, "For us it's exactly the same. I can stand outside our parliament building and shout, 'The American President is an idiot,' and nothing will happen to me!"

As we were thanking our guide and saying our goodbyes, Angela congratulated her on her language skills and asked if she'd studied English at school. "No, I learned English by watching MTV." That'll explain the accent then!

The only difficulty we had in navigating our way around Moscow was with the signage. As at the airport, the Cyrillic alphabet was a real stumbling block, and for much of the time we were only rescued by Angela's recognition of some of the letters from when she studied physics and somehow cobbling together what certain words may – or may not! – translate to.

All things considered, we coped very well. It was annoying to discover, however, that if our visit had been the following year, then much of the signage would've been in English as Russia geared up to host the World Cup in 2018! Ach well, we can say we got the authentic experience.

We were both blown away by Moscow, simply a beautiful, modern European city – we were even being offered a 5G signal on our phones before 5G existed in the UK! Things may have been different, and almost certainly still are, in the Russian hinterland, but as a capital city, Moscow is right up there with the best that we've experienced. There are many links between Scotland and Russia, not least sharing the same patron saint. Our hotel was in the same street as St Andrew's Church so, obviously, we had to pay that a wee visit, and we also just had to see Gorky Park – and not just to sing "Wind of Change"… though we did.

But the main sightseeing highlights were taking a closer look around Red Square, the Kremlin, St Basil's Cathedral, the Bolshoi Theatre, GUM – the giant department store that dates back to the tsars – and many of the museums and exhibitions around this wonderful city. But one unexpected bonus was the Moscow Metro – what a place! – where every station is like an ornate art gallery in an amazing contradiction to the fast, clean, ultra-modern train system that they service.

Our only regret was that we didn't schedule a longer break and visit St Petersburg in a twin-centre holiday. At the time, we consoled ourselves by thinking we'd definitely arrange that sometime, as well as return to Moscow because we'd enjoyed the city so much. However, world events since then have conspired to make any visit to Russia, sadly, unlikely for at least the foreseeable future.

Once again, we didn't have too long to wait until we were returning to *la bella Italia* and our "other life" but, before that, in one of our by now legendary "detours", we decided to visit friends "en route" to Nardelli. This particular episode of "we'll do that on the way" involved driving from Ijmuiden to Challignac in the Charente region of France...

Now, if you look at a map, Ijmuiden to Nardelli, directly going through the Netherlands, Germany and Austria, is pretty much a straight line south-east... Driving to Challignac, however, meant a 12-hour journey in a south-westerly direction to within an hour of the Bay of Biscay. We never learn!

Anyway, after an overnight stop on the outskirts of Paris, we made it to our friends' place the following day – a beautiful house but in the middle of absolutely nowhere. Having thought this journey through in writing this, I'm finding it hard to believe that we made that detour to see them then only stayed there for three nights. But it was good to see them, and their new place, even if we then had an even more daunting journey ahead, as Nardelli was still around 16 hours away.

Notwithstanding that slight inconvenience, it did offer us the opportunity for Angela to sample the Mont Blanc experience I'd had several years earlier with my dad.

After a long cross-country French trek, traversing the Massif Central, we rocked up in Annecy again – again for me that is – then on towards Mont Blanc the following morning. As I mentioned previously, it's a spectacular sight, and I was happy to finally be able to share that journey with Angela.

Once we emerged from the tunnel and could see Monte Bianco in our rear-view mirror – well, it's only fair to use its Italian name since it's jointly "owned" – it was onwards through Genoa and down past Pisa to eventually return to that "other life" in Umbria.

The summer progressed as it usually does, catching up with friends in Nardelli, Pozzuolo, Castiglione del Lago and elsewhere, interspersed with a few more touristy excursions to places like Siena, Firenze, Roma and the like. In August, we were off again to one of our favourite places, Sorrento, with our friends Ian and Carol, who were visiting us for a week.

Because it was their first time there, we took on the role of tourist guides around some places we now knew very well indeed. One day, we drove down the Amalfi coast, visiting Positano, Ravello and, naturally, Amalfi itself. Amalfi is always busy, but over the years, we've noticed it getting increasingly more crowded and, on this particular day, it was absolutely rammed with tourists. I already knew parking would be an issue, so I suggested that Angela, Carol and Ian got out at the main gateway and went exploring while I found a parking space – easier said than done.

I did multiple loops of the town – not easy as there's only one linear road along the coast – but there wasn't a single parking space to be found. By the way, this is the story I hinted at towards the end of Book 2 as, on this occasion, there only being one road in most certainly did not mean that nothing could go wrong…

All this time, Angela and I had been updating each other by text and had eventually decided that they should go for lunch and I'd join them when I could. However, by this time I'd been driving around fruitlessly for over an hour and, in desperate need of a toilet stop, decided to keep driving down the coast in search of a loo. I finally found a parking space in Maiori, a few towns and 5 km further down the coast! I went into the first hotel I saw and ordered a coffee, purely so I could visit their bathroom. I then phoned Angela to tell her I wasn't going to make lunch and I'd pick them up when they were ready – I have a great selfie of poor little me sitting on my lonesome at a bar on the seafront with an espresso and a croissant, while they were scooping it up in Amalfi.

When they were good to go, I drove back to pick them up, all suitably "refreshed" after being fed and watered – more beered and wined than watered actually! That only really dawned on me as we headed back towards Sorrento, as Angela and Carol were particularly giggly. I asked why they were having a "mad half hour", but Ian helpfully reminded me that they were a full carafe of wine ahead of me – well, that explains that then.

One evening, we all went out for a special dinner in a quaint little restaurant in the centre of Sorrento which has little grottos at the back of its garden area. It was a beautiful setting, and as we were settling in and perusing the menu, the owner approached and started telling us about his specials as well as making recommendations from the menu. On hearing that both Carol and I were vegetarians, he started to wax lyrical about a few dishes that weren't on the menu but he'd be happy to prepare for us.

Anyway, we all ordered things that were either specials or suggested by *il capo*, and as each course arrived, we were not disappointed. It was an excellent meal with great company in a beautiful location, so we all have great memories. In fact, the cover photo for this trilogy of books is based on a shot that Ian took, at Angela's suggestion, while we were messing around at the table – there were others that would not have been suitable!

The entertainment was a guitarist, and at some point he decided to serenade us, which the girls lapped up. For some reason though, he took a particular shine to me – no, not in *that* way – probably because Angela had told him I'd been "learning" to play the guitar for years and still hadn't mastered a single chord – harsh but true. Anyway, he asked what kind of music I liked then started playing stuff of whatever genre I'd said while looking me in the eye from a very close range – I found this both embarrassing and unnerving whereas the other three thought it was hilarious.

To round the evening off, *il capo* returned and offered us a *digestivo* of his own: home-made, chilli "viagroncello" – his little twist on the famous local limoncello – which he claimed was so powerful that only Ian and I could drink it. It wasn't for the ladies.

He returned with only two glasses, as promised, for us hardy men, and, of course, we were immediately mugged by our even hardier wives who insisted on trying this powerful aphrodisiac... It was tasty enough, I suppose, though not as hot chilli-wise as he'd claimed. And, more pertinently, it seemed to do absolutely nothing to make any of us "hot to trot" as claimed – that's about as politely as I can put it.

All great fun, and our memorable evening drew to a close when we discovered the results of having ordered so many recommendations and specials – a bill that was at least double what we expected. *Mamma mia*! Ach well, what price can you put on good times such as this?

Another memorable event from the summer of 2016 was, of course, the totally ludicrous and absolutely unnecessary vote on Brexit. I've always detested that framing – "Brexit" – as I think it trivialised the whole thing in some people's minds and actually contributed significantly to the outcome.

Planning ahead, we'd arranged a proxy vote for "Remain" and were convinced we would be on the winning side. When we read the news online on the morning after the vote, 24 June, we were in total shock and disbelief. The only good thing about it was that when we went to our local bar for morning coffee, many locals came over to us with their newspaper showing Scotland voting "Remain" while England voted "Leave" and said, "Now we understand!"

What they were referring to was the fact that ever since we'd arrived in Pozzuolo 10 years previously, we'd had to patiently explain to – and often vehemently argue with – anyone and everyone that we weren't English, we were Scottish, and that Scotland is a separate country with different morals and different attitudes. Finally, they got it!

That realisation, however, was cold comfort against what this Brexit vote could, and ultimately would, mean for us in regard to, well, just about everything really, and so it has come to prove.

One of our first actions on returning home was to start the process of Angela acquiring Italian citizenship through her grandfather, Lorenzo, who she'd never met as he'd died when her dad was a young adult. Much research followed and, bit by bit, we edged closer to completing a portfolio of evidence for her to confirm her citizenship, as Italian law stated clearly and categorically that foreign-born descendants of Italians were deemed to be Italian from birth and that the citizenship process was merely to confirm that the applicant was indeed Italian.

One sticking point for us was trying to prove that Lorenzo had never naturalised in Britain. It was only after Angela had received an official letter from the National Archives stating that there was "no evidence of naturalisation" did the penny finally drop – how can you prove that someone *didn't* do something? You can only prove that no evidence could be found that they *had* done something…

Getting to that conclusion took many, many months of agonising, and going down rabbit holes of family history research, all of which was very interesting but none of which was improving on what that official letter told us. Once that was clear in our minds, we could gather the other necessary documentation, have it legalised and translated, and arrange an appointment with the Italian Consulate in Edinburgh, which finally happened in 2018 – almost two full years after we'd started the process! At this point, we'll pause, once again, let the suspense build and await the outcome…

One final observation on the bureaucracy of the situation, from a Scottish perspective: if we require an official copy of our birth certificate, we can order one from the National

Records of Scotland, and, for a few pounds, a beautifully embossed certificate is delivered to our home within a week. However, to have that official certificate legally recognised, we have to send it to England so that our colonial masters can endorse it as "official" with what is effectively a sticker and charge mightily for the privilege. This is an absurdity, and an insult to the people of Scotland.

Soon enough, it was time to scoot off again to spend another festive period in Umbria. This time, Angela had decided to host Christmas Day for Neno and his family and introduce them to a traditional Scottish Christmas dinner. The extra surprise twist was provided by yours truly wearing full Highland dress for the day, and to say this went down well with our guests would be a severe understatement – they were absolutely delighted!

They even adapted reasonably well to having only three courses instead of six, and to having all of their main course on the same plate rather than the Italian norm of having the meat on one plate and the vegetables, *contorni*, served as a separate course on a separate plate. Strange or not, they fairly scoffed down the turkey and traditional trimmings – obviously yours truly had a vegetarian alternative to turkey – as well as the lentil soup starter and the Christmas pudding and custard dessert. It was a memorable day, though the good feelings weren't destined to last too long...

During the week between Christmas and New Year, Neno didn't seem like his usual self, though he didn't appear overly bothered by this and everything just went on as usual. We invited him to ours for another Scottish tradition, the steak pie dinner – we'd brought a veggie version for me – on Ne'erday, and he seemed to be looking forward to it.

When he didn't appear at the agreed time – his house is only 20 metres or so from ours – we went round to check on him, and he seemed a bit disorientated and confused about the time. Eventually, he managed to get himself organised and we set about our New Year celebrations a little later than planned, but he still didn't seem right.

We let his daughter, Donatella, know what had gone on, so she came to check on him the following day, and after a doctor's visit, he was taken to the local hospital for a few days of tests and observations. What followed was devastating news, which was withheld from us for a good while – essentially poor Neno was in the latter stages of the same illness that had taken his brother quite recently and all that could be done was purely palliative.

By this time, we were due to return to Scotland, and although everyone put on a brave face and talked about recovery, we all suspected that this was the last time we would see Neno. Once we were back home, we called him every few days, and he would seem cheery enough, though he was clearly getting weaker by the day. Latterly, we were the only people outwith his immediate family that he would even try to speak to, which underlined how deep a friendship we'd formed over the previous 10 years.

On the morning we were due to fly from Scotland to Mallorca to visit Angela's sister Ruth, Donatella called to say that her dad had passed. Italian tradition dictates that funerals happen very quickly, and even if we hadn't been en route to Mallorca, it would've been impossible for us to get to Umbria in time, so all we could do was send flowers and messages of condolence to the family and think of the happy times we'd spent together.

Nazzareno Bigi was a special man who, despite not understanding a word of English, had invited two Scots into his family and shared many good times with us. We even taught him a wee bit of Scots, and it still makes us smile when we recall overhearing him giggle and say "teeny-weeny" as he pulled out some tiny weeds…

Providing some distraction from that sadness was the visit to Mallorca and the opportunity to sample a bit of Angela's sister's new life with her Spanish partner, Juan. It was an enjoyable week as Juan guided us round various popular venues around the island, and despite the fact that we were there in February, we even had a few sunny days – one in particular was when we visited Palma, the capital, to have lunch with Angela's uncle Andy, who'd lived in Mallorca since 1963. We also met Juan's family and discovered there was no language barrier if they spoke Spanish, we spoke Italian and Juan translated the few bits that either side didn't quite understand.

Apart from a tearful reunion with Neno's family, there was nothing much to remember in particular about the summer of 2017 in Nardelli – apart from the usual fun in the sun and catch-ups with friends – although the contrast in temperature between that summer and our next trip away in November is certainly memorable…

Krakow in November is chilly, and taking the opportunity to visit Auschwitz was even more chilling. The story of the atrocities committed by the Nazis in this, and other, concentration camps is simply one of unfathomable evil. As I've said before, visiting these types of place is not, for me, tourism; it's a way of remembering and never forgetting what can happen when idealogues are allowed by us, the people, to get out of control.

That is something we should reflect very seriously on given the situation in the world today, not only in Palestine or Ukraine, but in all of the "armed conflicts" worldwide – at the point of writing this there are, apparently, more than 120. And yet, our politicians are seemingly only interested in fuelling the so-called "war machine" by pouring ever-increasing amounts of money into weaponry of all kinds. This is sheer madness, and they've clearly forgotten what this all leads to in terms of human suffering…

Krakow, however, is another beautiful and well-preserved city, and we were really happy to learn of its Scottish connections – in the 16th and 17th centuries, there were around 30,000 Scots living in Poland, and there are records which confirm Scottish merchants being granted citizenship of Krakow. Who knew? Well, certainly not us as, shamefully, we Scots were never taught Scottish history at school – a recurring theme.

A happier, though at least equally chilly, excursion took us to the Wieliczka salt mine, around half an hour outside Krakow. If at all possible, we always try to get to places independently, so we researched what bus we needed to catch and off we went. It was the first time I'd seen contactless payment on a bus, way before it was introduced in Scotland.

The tour was fascinating, with some incredibly intricate sculptures on display, and spending a couple of hours underground gave at least some kind of flavour – salty, of course – of what conditions must've been like for the miners, though I think it must've been a healthier environment than coal mining.

CHAPTER 10

The day before you came

(2018–2020)

So, earlier I left a wee tease about Angela's Italian citizenship application…

Having gathered together all of the necessary paperwork and jumped through all the bureaucratic hoops – or so we thought – an appointment was arranged at the Italian Consulate in Edinburgh for early March where she was due to hand over her documentation, pay the application fee and officially enter the process.

Now, remember that by this stage she'd had to assemble a portfolio of documents including birth, marriage and death certificates proving her Italian heritage from her grandfather through her father, and have each of these certificates legalised – in England! – then every single page translated by an official translator, none of which was exactly cheap. You can imagine our surprise, and disappointment, when the official looked through the portfolio and said, "But we haven't approved these translations."

What? Despite the translations being carried out by a translator on the consulate's approved list, it turned out that someone in the consulate had to confirm that the translations were indeed accurate... which incurred yet another fee, naturally.

We naïvely thought that he could do that there and then, but he seemed quite annoyed at the very suggestion – how very dare we! – and said that Angela would have to return for a second appointment once his colleague had approved the translations. Now, this posed a wee bit of a problem because we were due to leave for Italy again in May – I know, you're shocked at that revelation! – and fully expected him to arrange the return appointment for after we'd left. But after explaining our concerns, he reluctantly agreed to fit us in two weeks later – phew!

The second visit went very smoothly, and after he'd relieved Angela of her fee, he seemed to take just a wee bit too much pleasure in putting her file at the bottom of a very large pile of citizenship applications while reminding her that the process could now take up to two years.

Still, it was all very exciting that this was now finally in progress, so we tried to forget about it and turned our attentions to the summer of 2018. This was to include another of our "holidaymakers in our own country" experiences, as we'd agreed to fly home for a week in early June to attend the wedding of Carol and Ian's daughter, Sara.

The previous year, Ian had asked me if I would write, and perform, a humorous poem in place of his father-of-the-bride speech – he was worried about making a speech himself as, by this time, motor neurone disease was starting to affect his ability to speak. The thought terrified me! But how could I say no to my good friend? And it was very flattering to be asked – an honour in fact.

We'd had a few conversations about funny – and preferably embarrassing – stories about Sara's childhood and suchlike, which I then weaved into a hopefully funny but definitely irreverent poem to conclude the speeches on her big day. I'll just say again, I was terrified! Anyway, cometh the hour cometh the man, and a very nervous Gordon somehow managed to steel himself and, apparently confidently, deliver the poem pretty much flawlessly.

It was well received, particularly by the principal "targets" – Sara, her brother Donald and bridegroom Matt – and, importantly, by both Carol and Ian. Angela later told me that she could see my hands shaking while I was reciting the poem, though that hadn't come across in my voice, and I was just extremely happy, and relieved, when it was all over. The week had passed very quickly, and soon we were back in Umbria ready to enjoy the rest of the summer.

However, best-laid plans and all that… Life had other ideas, and I unexpectedly ended up in hospital in Perugia only a few days later.

At this point, dear reader, if you know, you know, and if you don't, then you probably don't need to – I did say right at the start that I wasn't divulging everything. Suffice to say, the Italian health service took great care of me, and the doctors and nurses, firstly in the A&E department of Castiglione del Lago Hospital and then at the much larger Perugia Hospital, commonly referred to as Silvestrini, were absolutely fantastic. They saved my life, aided and abetted by my long-standing vegetarianism and physical fitness I believe, but the less said about my family history, the better.

Workwise, 2018 included a great leap forward for my still-fledgling career as an author/journalist/feature-writer, as

I was invited into the *iScot Magazine* family by its remarkable founder, Ken McDonald. We hit it off right away on a personal level, and as the magazine is unashamedly pro-Scotland and pro-independence, the opportunity to research and produce articles on a variety of themes was just what I needed.

I've learned so many things about Scotland's history, politics and culture, none of which were even referred to never mind taught in schools until very, very recently. I've mentioned previously that I've always been convinced of the case for the restoration of Scotland's independence, but the sheer volume of the discoveries I've made during my reading and researching for the magazine has reinforced that long-held conviction. As I said before, Scotland is the last remaining colony of the English/British Empire, nothing will ever convince me otherwise, and this travesty of justice has to change – *Alba gu bràth*!

Unlike Angela's approach to "landmark" birthdays, I tend to be a bit more understated and see them as "just another day" – I don't mean that in a killjoy way; I just think that every day, and every birthday, is special... I'm not explaining that too well really! Anyway, we eventually came up with a plan for April 2019 and decided to incorporate my birthday into a tour of the North Coast 500 – the NC500 was launched in 2015 as a "brand" with the aim of promoting the 500-ish miles of coastline around the top of mainland Scotland, starting and finishing at Inverness.

However, this plan clearly wasn't enough for my scheming wife, so, on the sly, she sneakily arranged for a few friends to gather for a surprise birthday lunch – a few days before my birthday – followed by a visit to our local escape rooms. Not only did I suspect nothing, I didn't even know

Dundee had such a facility, nor was I really all that clued up on what we had to do and, as it turned out, I was probably the least useful participant. It was all very enjoyable though, even if they'd all conspired behind my back…

Meanwhile, back at the NC500… We decided to go anticlockwise and, after an overnight stay in Inverness, drove over the Kessock Bridge, across the Black Isle, skirting Dingwall, then up through Tain, Golspie, Brora, Helmsdale, Wick, and John o' Groats before concluding our first day in Castletown, just outside Thurso – a hell of a first day! We stopped at various places en route – for instance, Dunrobin Castle, where we mused that the aristocracy were never "done robbin'" us! – but our principal unexpected find was at Helmsdale, a place we were shamefully unaware of.

We only stopped because Angela spotted an interesting-looking sculpture at the side of the road, so we parked and explored. It turns out, the Emigrants Statue is a memorial to those Scots evicted from their homes during the Highland Clearances and is of infinitely more significance than the nearby statue of the Duke of Sutherland, "The Mannie", which blights Ben Bhraggie and "commemorates" an entitled English landowner largely responsible for those clearances!

Further up the road, we were intrigued by a random sign we spotted so diverted up a wee side road to discover the Hill o' Many Stanes, near Lybster, which consists of around 200 small stones arranged in 22 rows, and apparently from about 4,000 years ago. Nobody seems to know too much definitive about them, but they were possibly placed for gatherings or religious ceremonies. This was a fascinating and, again, totally unexpected wee find.

Our next target was the more famous Duncansby Stacks, a spectacular sight, then on to John o' Groats, which was slightly disappointing – apart from the iconic sign, what else is there? Anyway, from John o' Groats we scooted along the road in search of Dunnet Head, Scotland's most northerly mainland point. As we stood there looking out across the wild waters of the North Atlantic Ocean, it was somehow quite emotional, and humbling, to think that the next land in that north-westerly direction would be Iceland and Greenland.

Our hotel in Castletown was definitely a classic example of "faded glory" and had long since attained the status of being more shabby than chic, like far too many small-town, traditional Scottish hotels unfortunately. Still, it was only for one night, and it wasn't too bad really, though waking up the following morning as a 60-year-old – did I just admit that? – in those less than glamorous surroundings was a little deflating. Ach, not really, after all I was celebrating my "landmark" birthday with my soulmate and we had an exciting day ahead as we continued our jaunt along the top edge of our beautiful country...

After a decent birthday breakfast – the old-school silver service contrasting wildly with the duct-taped carpeting – we doubled back on ourselves for a quick visit to the Dunnet Bay Distillery before continuing onwards to Thurso. Now, uppermost in my mind was to remember to fill up with petrol before leaving Thurso because I wasn't sure how many refuelling opportunities lay ahead.

But, not for the first time, I got distracted – no surprise there for Angela! Because she had to post something – there's me starting to shift the blame – we parked in the town centre and tried to locate the post office, which we eventually did, then went back to the car and drove on with all thoughts of refuelling magically gone.

I only remembered about 10 minutes later, at which point I naïvely decided that returning to Thurso was a waste of valuable time and we were bound to see a petrol station somewhere soon…

By this time, we were approaching Dounreay where, if you remember the very first page of Chapter 1, Book 1, was where it all started – literally – for the birthday boy. That also felt a bit odd, even though, obviously, I wasn't actually there when it all began, but it did seem like a bit of a full circle moment.

Whatever emotions I was feeling, however, were quickly set aside as I didn't think it was wise to hang around a decommissioned nuclear power station any longer than was absolutely necessary. So we sped on, with my attention constantly flickering between the increasingly sparse landscape and the ever-diminishing petrol gauge…

We were blessed with another beautifully sunny day, and the features of that landscape were fascinating and so different from what we're accustomed to where we live. Our next stopping-off point was to be Smoo Cave – petrol permitting! – and it was a great relief when we arrived there, and an even greater relief when we spotted a single self-serve petrol pump just up the road.

After wandering around the waterfall chamber in the cave, we refuelled – phew! – and headed on to Durness in a far more relaxed frame of mind. There were two things we wanted to see in Durness: the fancy high-end chocolatier (!) and the cemetery where one of John Lennon's aunties, Elizabeth, is buried. After overindulging in fancy chocolate, washed down with fancy hot chocolate, we attempted to walk off the effects in the cemetery and on the famous beach.

We didn't find any sign of Elizabeth's grave, so we walked out the back of the cemetery directly on to the wide, golden sands of Durness beach, which is stunning. All the while though, we could hear loud bangs in the distance – live firing on the MoD range at Cape Wrath. We had hoped to include a visit to Cape Wrath on our tour, as it's the most north-westerly point of mainland Scotland, but we couldn't find any information online as to how to get there.

When we were in the chocolatier's, we asked how we could get to Cape Wrath only to be told that we couldn't because of the MoD... It was only possible at certain times, but only by ferry and bus and for a short period. What? It's a complete disgrace that the north-west corner of our country has been stolen by the British military and that we're denied access to our own land – I'm still furious about that.

Setting that fury aside, we turned "downhill" towards our next destination, Lochinver. Some of the landscape on this section of the journey was like the surface of the moon – not literally, obviously – and it was difficult to equate it to the Scotland we know. After a lovely afternoon taking in the ever-changing scenery, we arrived at a cosy little B&B in Lochinver, with a great view over the town and the loch below. We were particularly pleased to see the Saltire flying on the terrace, and after settling in, we were happy to crack open the Prosecco and celebrate my birthday under that bonnie blue flag, with Loch Inver as a scenic backdrop.

Next day, we were up bright and early for the next leg and, after a hearty breakfast, set off to take in Ullapool, Poolewe, Gairloch, Shieldaig, then elected to take the coast road to Applecross. Again, simply stunning views, and on the last section, that coast road, having to navigate around several basking Highland Cows that freely wander about on the road was an interesting experience.

Applecross was good to see, though there's not really much to it, so we took off again towards the challenge that is Bealach na Bà, one of the highest passes in Scotland – amazingly, only the third-highest – and the narrowness of the road combined with the tight bends and steep slopes certainly demands full concentration, particularly when you see a camper van hurtling towards you! Even so, there are plenty of opportunities to take in the views, and despite the bright April sunshine, there were still pockets of snow visible.

With that Bealach na Bà box ticked, we were now heading to our next overnight stop at Stromeferry after circumnavigating Loch Carron. We were intrigued by a sign we spotted on arrival – Strome Ferry (no ferry) – and when we arrived at that night's B&B, the owners explained that there used to be a ferry but it had been discontinued in 1970 after the road we'd just arrived on had been completed around Loch Carron. They asked what our plans were, and when we said we intended to visit Eilean Donan Castle the following day, they recommended we drive to it once darkness fell as it was a completely different experience at night – great advice, and it certainly was! After a good night's sleep and another hearty breakfast, we returned to the castle in the morning and spent an interesting hour or so touring it and learning its fascinating history.

Then it was off towards Spean Bridge and on to Glenfinnan to see where the Jacobite standard had been raised in 1745. We climbed the hill to see the famous viaduct from above, but, unfortunately, there was to be no steam train passing that day. The view was fantastic mind, as was the view over the Jacobite monument and Loch Shiel. Then it was on to Fort William, and a glimpse of Ben Nevis, before heading to our next overnighter on the shores of Loch Lomond.

Effectively then, that was our take on the NC500 over, and the following day we drove down to Helensburgh to have lunch with Ken, the *iScot Magazine* owner, before turning eastwards and heading for home. A whistle-stop tour indeed, but a memorable way to commemorate a memorable birthday – yet again, good times!

For our summer sojourn south, we took a slightly different route this year, staying overnight near Pforzheim, where we'd spotted a good deal in what appeared to be a conference centre in some beautiful parkland. The Hohenwart Forum was indeed a conference centre but one with distinctly religious overtones, which was unexpected… and a wee bit spooky.

Post-visit research would confirm that it "has a strong connection to Christianity, specifically Protestantism" and that other guests had commented on the vibe of "Christian propaganda" with one saying, "I felt as if the Protestant message was being forced upon me" – oops, maybe some more intensive *pre*-visit research would've been beneficial.

Anyway, we were only to be there for one night, so we retreated to our sparsely furnished, almost monastic – but comfortable enough – room and forgot about our unexpectedly pious surroundings.

One of the domestic German customs that I've really come to appreciate over the years is that of having individual duvets on the double beds. The justification for this practice is that it eliminates "duvet stealing" during the night and also allows for different ratings to be used dependent on each individual's internal thermostat – genius!

Anyway – and I have special permission from the boss to share this story – as we settled in to sleep and I was doing my usual wriggling around, bedding myself in, as it were – a habit which Angela likens to a dog getting comfy in its basket – I said, "Ah, I'd forgotten how good it is having your own duvet, what a great idea... Mind you, I have absolutely no idea where mine is!" – I'd obviously kicked it off during my personal wriggle-fest – "but I don't suppose it matters when I've got my own personal Baxi boiler strapped to my chest."

At this, Angela then disintegrated into uncontrollable laughter, setting me off too, which meant that sleep was delayed until our convulsions subsided. If anyone under the age of 50 is confused by this anecdote, ask an older woman.

Yet another summer of Umbrian fun and frolics included a wee bit of work when I decided to pitch a couple of articles to a few newspapers and magazines. Now, this is a fairly soul-destroying process as, more often than not, they don't even bother to answer.

One reply fair tickled me though – and also raised my hackles in pretty much equal measure. I'd written a humorous – I thought! – piece about the peculiarities of Italian driving. When I saw that I'd received an email from a features editor at a major Sunday newspaper, I was initially excited, right up until I read Ms Double-Barrelled Snooty Bitch's verdict:

This is the most bizarre story I've ever been sent! Thanks for entertaining us, but we would never run something like this... sorry.

What? Apart from clearly having had a sense of humour bypass, I seriously doubt that she'd read it properly – she certainly hadn't taken much time over writing that response as what you've just read has been severely edited by me in terms of spelling, grammar and punctuation!

I replied:

> *Thanks for getting back to me, I think! I'm not sure exactly how you would justify describing my piece as "bizarre"? It's a well written, tongue-in-cheek account of a quirky subject, based on personal experience, that has been well received by quite a few editors. Clearly, you've decided it's not right for your publication, but that is no reason to send such an unprofessional response.*

That wis her telt! To be fair, she did come back again, a little conciliatory... I think:

> *OK, sorry, Gordon! Maybe I should've said "quirky". Thanks for sending it anyway. It's just too close to being xenophobic for us to run at* The Guardian...

Again, I've had to clean up her writing – how that is acceptable at *The Guardian* is a mystery to me! – but "xenophobic"? That couldn't be any further from the truth. At this point, if she'd decided she was interested, I would have told her to "get tae..." and to keep her snooty, yet somehow illiterate, opinions to herself.

Swiftly putting that quirkily bizarre interchange behind me, I then offered it to an English-language Italian magazine, *The Local Italy*, and they happily published it. I've received several positive reviews of the piece over the years, including one very recently as it's still available online.

They also published another piece I'd written about our local town, Pozzuolo, where I praised the quality of our friend Salvatore's coffee in Bar Controvento. When I proudly showed him the article, I expected him to be chuffed, but his immediate downbeat reaction was just, "You didn't mention my ice cream." Ach well, you can please some of the people some of the time...

Early August brought our friend Donatella's 50th birthday celebration, where her daughters presented her with a gift of a city break in Amsterdam at the start of September. When we realised this could coincide handily with our journey back home, we arranged things so that we could meet up for a day.

Angela booked us on the Amsterdam Botel, a former cruise ship which has been converted to a floating hotel in the IJ, Amsterdam's waterfront. It's a sensational location and a unique experience, with a free ferry service 250 metres away running every 15 minutes to Amsterdam Centraal Station – I say "unique", but for us it was exactly the same as the cabin on the ferry from Ijmuiden to Newcastle that we'd been using for years, albeit without the often-choppy conditions of the North Sea. Anyway, it was a perfect base for exploring Amsterdam again and for meeting up with Dona.

In keeping with our nautical theme, we had dinner in the Sea Palace, the floating Chinese restaurant docked a short distance from Centraal Station – this is the restaurant I mentioned in the previous book when we almost died of hypothermia when we visited one February, with -18°C temperatures. Thankfully, the September weather was much kinder...

After an afternoon wandering around "the Dam" together, as we were approaching the Sea Palace, we saw three guys attempting to take a selfie with the restaurant boat in the background. We asked if they'd like one of us to take the photo instead, and when they replied, it was obvious they were also Scottish – more than that, one was from Dundee! Here's tae us. Wha's like us? We fairly get around…

After that brief recreation of our Umbrian life in Amsterdam, the following day we were back on a boat – moving this time – to return home and begin planning our next trip, which would be for Angela's birthday in November. She booked a shepherd's hut just outside Dufftown, and despite the inevitably freezing weather, we made every attempt to celebrate her birthday in style.

One of the features that had attracted Angela to this hut was the firepit on the decking overlooking a valley with Dufftown in the near distance. Her "dream" was to be sipping Prosecco and toasting marshmallows on the firepit while taking in the view – oh dear, the reality was to prove somewhat different.

The owner had delivered logs for the firepit while we were out exploring Findhorn Bay on the afternoon of Angela's birthday, but, unfortunately, she hadn't left them undercover and… it rained. Of course it did! We tried everything to get the fire going, but the damp wood was definitely making combustion difficult, if not impossible, so I decided to nip into Dufftown in search of firelighters.

Fifteen minutes later, an entire box of firelighters had the flames leaping into the evening sky, but we soon discovered that an entire box of firelighters tends to lend a somewhat toxic chemical flavour to toasted marshmallows!

We quickly gave up on the marshmallows, but Angela wasn't letting her Prosecco-by-firelight vision go that easily, and despite the fire beginning to die down – it turned out that only the firelighters and paper were actually burning; the logs were just steaming slightly – we have photographic evidence that she celebrated her birthday on the decking firepit burning, Prosecco in hand… with her parka hood up, offering only slight protection against the – by now – driving hailstones.

Photoshoot over, it was time to retreat to the centrally-heated shepherd's hut with the untoasted toxin-free marshmallows and finish off the Prosecco. An object lesson in how things don't have to go perfectly, and rarely do, in order to forge happy memories.

Talking of fire, to celebrate Hogmanay, we decided to drive up to the Comrie Flambeaux, their annual fire festival, to see in the New Year, and it was excellent. We followed that up on Ne'erday by driving through to Falkirk for the Fire and Light Festival at the Kelpies – there's definitely a fire theme emerging here.

The Kelpies are a magnificent sight in any conditions, but with the lighting at the festival, and all around Helix Park too, it was a truly sensational evening and an excellent way to celebrate the start of 2020. Little did we know what was to come…

Even when we headed back to Edinburgh at the end of January, for the anti-Brexit demonstration outside the Scottish Parliament, we were still in the dark about how this year was going to pan out. In mid-February, we hosted our friend Des, over from Waterford for a few days, showing him the sights of Dundee and Angus and having a generally fantastic time, but bits and pieces of news about this strange virus that had apparently been imported into Italy from China – Covid – were gaining traction.

Information, and a growing sense of concern, was changing on a daily basis, but it soon became clear that something extremely dangerous was going on worldwide – not that you would know from the clown show running Westminster at that time. Anyway, we had one really important thing to do as we entered March, and that was to drive through to Edinburgh to collect Angela's Italian passport from the consulate.

When her citizenship had been confirmed by email in mid-January, she'd immediately completed her passport application. A few weeks later, they'd emailed to say the passport was ready for collection, so we arranged an appointment on 2 March – my mum and dad's wedding anniversary – still without knowing exactly what lay ahead. What we did know was that Angela had now honoured her grandfather's heritage by gaining Italian citizenship, while simultaneously reacquiring her European citizenship.

Now, it should've been my turn, but the universe had other plans…

As the pandemic approached ever closer to home, and with warnings from our Italian friends coming in thick and fast, we decided to enter our own personal lockdown before the official guidance was issued. Our last "event" pre-Covid was at Tannadice to see United play Partick Thistle, on 7 March. By then it was clear that there would be some kind of official lockdown announced shortly, so we just decided to pre-empt that and hunker down early – the official restrictions came into force on 24 March, by which time we were only concerned with Scottish Government advice and completely ignoring Clown Prince Johnson and his incompetent, and corrupt, gang of charlatans in London.

At the start – apart from the ever-present threat of contracting a life-threatening virus every time you left the house – life continued pretty much as normal for us. Since we both worked from home, and any client dealings were remote anyway, day-to-day life was much the same as ever.

Initially, not being able to see friends wasn't nice, but once restrictions were slackened a little bit and we were able to socialise outdoors in "bubbles", some semblance of normality returned. The fact that this period coincided with amazingly good weather helped, as did a good dose of Scottish dark humour – we always recall how quickly the traditional greeting of, "How's it going?" quickly changed to, "Whit part o' two f★★★ing metres are you no' getting?"

As the summer progressed and the Westminster lunatics announced the great "eat out to help out" scheme – which, ridiculous though it was, we all enthusiastically embraced – we then went through the pantomime of donning masks to enter a restaurant, removing them while seated, putting them back on if we visited the toilet or any time we moved from the table. Why exactly was this virus so dangerous if it couldn't attack you when seated? Or had the UK Government just got that wrong too?

I mentioned earlier that after Angela's Italian citizenship had been confirmed, our attention turned to my route to acquiring citizenship by marriage, *Jure Matrimonii*. Thanks (?) to a recent change in the law, aside from gathering, legalising and translating all of my relevant documents, there was an important first step that had to be undertaken – a language exam... Gulp!

Prior to 2018, this wouldn't have been necessary, but now, without this important piece of paper – a certificate of proficiency in the Italian language at the European B1 standard – there wasn't any point in document gathering as everything else was only deemed to be valid if it was issued within six months of the application.

Previously, it had been possible to sit this exam in Edinburgh, but we quickly established this was no longer possible and that the closest venue now was Durham University – Durham! I've already explained the ridiculousness of having to get Scottish documentation "approved" by an English body, but the fact it was no longer possible to even sit this exam in Scotland was another twist in the tale.

Our fury was rendered pointless in any case as we quickly ascertained that, because of Covid, the exam wasn't on offer anywhere in the world because of the need for a face-to-face conversation as part of it...

Looking on the bright side, this delay at least gave me the opportunity to bring my Italian language skills up to the appropriate standard as, up until this point, although I could hold my own in some quite complicated Italian conversations, I was usually operating almost exclusively with nouns, and verbs were a complete mystery to me.

Angela had frequently chastised me about this and, on one memorable occasion, had shouted at me, "You have to learn how to conjugate!" to which I replied, "I don't know what you mean. I cannae even conjugate in English, so whit chance do I have in Italian?"

Now, there is, obviously, an element of exaggeration in that, for comic effect, as not being grammatically literate would make both writing and journalism a little difficult

– though, when you read certain newspapers, you might wonder. I remember being taught grammar all the way through primary school, but I really do think it peaked in P7 as I seriously don't remember any grammar lessons in secondary school.

I think that, in your native language, once you've learned the "rules", then you just apply them naturally and never go back to label tenses or any of the other grammatical components. Angela actually agrees and reckons she only became more aware of certain grammatical constructs in the English language when she was studying French – if you recall earlier stories, my French prowess had been holed beneath the waterline by the infamous Miss Doig, so I didn't have that experience.

Anyway, I tried a couple of things online, a few textbooks and a few CDs, without making too much progress, and then along came Duolingo. This was a fantastic discovery, and I was making great progress until a certain point, where the explanations seemed insufficient, and I started to lose heart a little.

However, being a highly qualified and experienced educationalist – he said modestly – I decided to design my own programme, reflecting how we all learned our native language in the first place. I mean, we all turned up at school at five years old able to construct reasonable sentences and hold conversations, and I don't expect many parents were focusing overly on conjugation?

I adopted a rote learning approach, with constant repetition of fairly basic Duolingo lessons until they became second nature, then moving along – rinse and repeat. I kept at this all the way through 2020, never missing a day of practice – well, we were in lockdown most of the time, so there wasn't much else to do – and continued up until the exam in… Well, that's a wee surprise for later…

Our working days, as I mentioned earlier, hadn't really changed during lockdown – Angela was busy working away on a steady stream of copy-editing projects, while my time was taken up with features for both *iScot Magazine* and the *Costco Connection*. Well, I say "my time was taken up", but obviously it wasn't being adequately taken up for Angela's liking.

One day, she asked what I was doing with my book, and when I replied in my customary, "Well, I don't know, I'm not sure, I'll need to have another look…" she exploded in a manner very similar to that when I was hesitating over buying the house in Italy.

"Look, if you're not going to get it published, then you've just wasted 10 years, so either get it finished or give it up!" Ouch!

I know when it's pointless arguing, and, in truth, she was right enough. I really am an exceptionally good procrastinator at the best of times – in fact, procrastination is high up on my skillset list, probably just behind my legendary indecision – and this book project was proving to be no exception.

To be fair, my propensity for procrastination could take a while to explain and may involve delving into all kinds of "ologies" that I don't really understand. You see, I'm quite expert at the art of procrastination, and I'm sure it's so deep rooted in my psyche that it's probably something I just have to accept – much harder for those around me, of course, but there may also be a genetic factor at work. When I was growing up, whenever my long-suffering mum would politely and patiently (or not?) enquire as to when some long-overdue household task might possibly be started, completed or both, my dad's standard response was always, "When the spirit moves." Now that's expert procrastination in action – or maybe that should be inaction?

Anyway, true enough, every so often, and usually around midnight, he would declare that now was indeed the time, and furniture would be cleared, walls would be stripped and all sorts of activity would take place, resulting in entire rooms being redecorated deep into the night. My job was usually to clean the paste off the table, which I hated as it was always cold and sticky and, all things considered, I'd really much rather have been in bed, but needs must and all that. The problem was, if he didn't finish in one go, there was absolutely no guarantee that the aforementioned spirit would still either be in residence or even remotely inclined to continue moving the next day, and hence we could be left with a partly decorated room until the next manifestation of said spirit. It must've driven my mum batty, which at least gives me some insight into how Angela must feel when I'm re-enacting this scene in a variety of contexts.

Anyway, with my ears still ringing from that, ahem, pep talk, I set to work figuring out what I had to do to complete the book. On revisiting the manuscript, I did get a refreshing sense of accomplishment in what had been achieved so far, but I also realised how much still had to be done to get it ready for publication.

My first realisation was that there was too much content for one book, or it would end up looking like *War and Peace*! The second was that the story ended in 2012... unsurprisingly, as that's where I'd stopped my "stream-of-consciousness" first draft. Hmm.

After a bit of thought, I realised that the initial story arc had a natural ending around the time my school and university days finished, and as a fortunate coincidence, that also provided a good number of words and pages for a readable book. Buoyed by this revelation, I ploughed on with renewed enthusiasm – editing, adding, recrafting and generally "polishing" – and managed to pull together what I thought was a decent effort by late summer.

Angela worked her editorial magic on the manuscript, and after a wee bit more tweaking, I was ready to release my "baby" for typesetting and turn around 60,000 words into a book.

Ken McDonald, who'd constantly encouraged me with the project, enthusiastically offered to publish under the iScot Media imprint, so all I now needed to do was finalise the cover concept. I'd visualised from the outset that I wanted to use a slightly hazy black-and-white version of a photo Ian Bain had taken in Sorrento on the front cover, with a heavy shadow like Robert Freeman had used on the *With the Beatles* album back in 1963. I also wanted that Beatles theme to continue on the back cover, using four different images of my coupon across the ages arranged like the *Let It Be* album cover but also incorporating that same shadow effect.

Ken organised a designer for me, and it would be fair to say that we experienced "creative differences" (!) as I tried to have my vision realised – but we got there in the end.

Another important task running alongside all of this page and cover design stuff was to secure permissions to use the lyrical extracts from The Beatles' "In My Life" and "Paperback Writer" and also Talking Heads' "Once in a Lifetime". The Beatles rights were reasonably straightforward to purchase from Sony/ATV, but the Talking Heads' experience was a little trickier, with no fewer than four different copyright owners across two geographic areas. Again, we got there in the end.

At some point in the whole publishing process, it made sense to me to try and pick a specific date for publication, something meaningful, and as November was almost upon us, we decided to aim for 30 November, St Andrew's Day. And so it came to pass – that sounds possibly a wee bit too grandiose – that *How Did I Get Here?: Rebel Without a Clue!* was officially unleashed into a still unsuspecting world on 30 November 2020.

It was a hugely exciting – and slightly terrifying! – experience for me, but only slightly less terrifying than the repercussions from my beautiful wife if I hadn't finally done it. I'm joking, of course. The whole thing wouldn't have been possible without her support and encouragement – gentle and not-so-gentle – and I know she was equally proud when the book was actually in our hands and on the shelves. I'm certain Mum, Dad and Tommy were looking down proudly too, even if they would almost certainly have been thinking, *He's been and gone and done whit?*

EPILOGUE

Paperback writer (act III)

(2025)

Never mind the "difficult second album", just wait until you reach the third! This has been the most difficult book of the trilogy to write, and I'm not entirely sure why. Is it because, in a strange kind of way, more recent memories are somehow harder to write about? Or is it just because they are more recent that there's more possibility of inadvertently causing someone hurt? I don't know, but it's definitely been trickier. Maybe it's just that, on rereading the manuscript, it often feels more like a travelogue than a memoir… but I'm thinking that's a good thing, as it shows that the minutiae and daily grind of work have been overtaken by adventures, fun and lots of laughter.

And so we've arrived at the end of Volume 3, another 20 years further into the story, but are we any nearer to me answering my own question, *How Did I Get Here?* Yes, we are. My story hasn't finished yet – and hopefully not for a long time! – but I think I've arrived at the answer I was searching for…

Before revealing that answer, however, here's a wee digression – surely not? – to try and explain what this whole project has been like. You probably won't be overly surprised to learn that not everything you've read, or are about to read, has been effortlessly recalled from the depths of my brain. Some memories came easier than others in absolutely crystal-clear detail, others were just snippets that required further research and many had been long forgotten until triggered by that research. And, as previously explained, I still managed to forget things, often quite important things, until after the books had been published… and yes, that'll be the case again with this one.

Even up to the point of writing this epilogue, I had a vague recollection of having written something way back at the start, in 2012, that I felt would be important to my story arc as it was obviously part of that initial "stream-of-consciousness" outpouring that kicked the whole project off. But did I know where it was or what it was? Did I chook! And then a wee bit of inspiration struck, and I searched through some old and long-forgotten files, and there it was, my original idea for the epilogue. I've edited it a wee bit and updated it where necessary, but I definitely think it deserves its place here…

So, after 30 chapters, three prologues and now the third epilogue, I think I've found the answer to *How Did I Get Here?*, but the one question still rattling around in my head is: *What have I learned from life in general and from this experience in particular?* Phew, there's a biggie! And I'm not sure I can answer that fully yet, but let's have a go…

The process of writing these books has been cathartic to some extent, recalling memories and, probably for the first time, placing different happenings in a more all-encompassing context than I've ever attempted before. Does that make sense? I think as we go through life, we may, but only may, be aware of the obvious juxtaposition of immediately before and after certain events but give little thought to a wider context. Some of this thinking begins to sound alarmingly like a mid-life crisis, but it's not – though I must admit to being increasingly, and strangely, drawn to clothing brands from my youth – ergo my recent purchase of a Ben Sherman suit – and I finally tracked down a pair of round Ray Ban sunglasses in order to channel the John Lennon look… but the search for the perfect Chelsea boot still goes on.

No, with the year we've just had [remember, this part was originally written in 2012…], I think it's only natural to be a little reflective and to want to remember, and clarify, things from the past. History is important, not necessarily as a predictor of the future but certainly as an explanation of the present. Wow, that's deep!

A great quote that keeps coming into my head just now is that "the past is a foreign country; they do things differently there". And that is so, so true! Writing this, and dredging up long-forgotten details from the recesses of my memory, has been a humbling experience but also a little like it all happened to someone else, somewhere else. Was I really that person? Did that really happen to me? Some things I've been able to recount with very little emotional attachment, like I was describing someone else. Yet other events are still so real, so vivid even though years have passed that I've felt like I was still living through them and that yes, I was and still am that person. Strange.

My overwhelming feeling is that I've not done too badly. I wouldn't say I've got everything right, but I can certainly rationalise and understand all the decisions I made at critical points. Would I make all the same decisions again? Possibly not but, faced with the same information in the same contexts again, then… probably. Would I change some things? Yes, if I could, absolutely. But without getting too deeply philosophical about it, where do you start with the changes?

Whatever changes you could make would affect the whole timeline afterwards, and some of the really good stuff may never have happened. Suppose I hadn't played football or had a chewing gum habit, would I have ever met Angela? Or second time around, what if I'd never sent that Christmas card?

Do I believe in fate? Maybe, but I think actions and consequences are possibly a little more random than that. I do, however, believe that we, Angela and I, were meant to be, and I'm grateful that we took our second chance irrespective of any random celestial activity. I feel blessed that I've been loved by, and have loved, beautiful people in my life and that their love has shaped me into the person I am today. And that love still drives me on to whatever comes next for us.

So, what's the plan? The plan is… there is no plan! But there are aspirations. Obviously, though true even if a little clichéd, these aspirations include continuing to be healthy and happy, but also to live life on our own terms. Whatever we're about to do will, ideally, continue to be time and location independent and allow us to continue to grow as people. It's what our parents prepared us for, and it's what we've prepared ourselves for. Recounting my – our – history in this book allows me to tick off that particular piece of reflection as "job done", and is the perfect preparation for moving on.

Do I understand myself more? I think so. I recognise both my strengths and my weaknesses, and I'm happy to say that the good by far outweighs the bad. Not that that was ever in doubt, of course (!), but actually recognising and analysing my flaws means I can attempt to rectify some, make allowances for others and live with the remainder… unless Angela beats them all out of me, which is always a possibility. I'm far too modest to list my strengths…

One hurdle that's already been overcome simply by arriving at this point is that I've finally proven to myself, at the very least, that I can write. It may be rubbish – I hope not – but I'm rapidly closing in on 200,000 words, and I'm pretty sure that not just everybody can do that. Popular opinion has it that you should write about what you know, so, in that respect at least, this should've been a scoosh – after all, if you don't know what your life's been about, what do you know? But is that true? How many people actually do know what their life's been about, and how many take the time or have the opportunity to think about it? I can absolutely recommend the experience.

It's strange to think that I wrote most of that section 13 or 14 years ago, yet the conclusions I arrived at still appear perfectly valid now, reinforced if anything.

And finally… I think that the answer to my question, *How Did I Get Here?*, is very, very simple, and I'm surprised and delighted to realise that I'd already got there when I wrote that draft epilogue above. *How Did I Get Here?* – love. That's it, one word, love. After getting on for 200,000 words spread over 600+ pages, that's it… love is the answer.

I've been blessed with a loving childhood and upbringing by my family and been fortunate enough to meet my soulmate and continue my journey surrounded by, and guided by, love. This story is at least as much about each of them as it is about me. Because the truth is that without them, there is no me – or certainly not the "me" I've come to understand. And I think I do have a better understanding of who I am, including the parts of me that often appear confusingly contradictory even to me.

Having kicked off with a quote from a Beatles' song that inspired the whole project, "In My Life", it's only right that I finish with a quote from another one – appropriately enough from "The End". Because in the end:

the love you take is equal to the love you make…

But is there a fourth part of the trilogy still to come? Well, even if the original question has been answered, the story hasn't ended – not to mention all the stuff I've missed out, again! – so I guess the answer to that is *yes*, though probably in a different form. Apart from anything else, that Italian citizenship journey has been left hanging… What a tease!

Printed in Dunstable, United Kingdom

83385243R00129